Feudalism, Capitalism and Beyond

H.E. Hallam
Eugene Kamenka
C.B. Macpherson
R.S. Neale
J.G.A. Pocock
Alice Erh-Soon Tay
F.J. West

The illustration on the cover and jacket depicts Capital as portrayed in
a twelfth-century manuscript. Reproduced in F.I. Bulgakov,
Illustrirovannaia istoriia knigopechataniia i tipograficheskogo iskusstva,
St Petersburg, 1889.

Feudalism, Capitalism
and Beyond

Feudalism, Capitalism and Beyond

Edited by
Eugene Kamenka and R.S. Neale

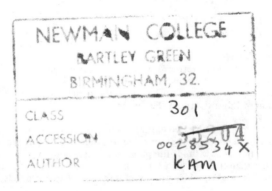

Edward Arnold

First published in Great Britain 1975 by
Edward Arnold (Publishers) Ltd
25 Hill Street, London W1X 8LL

ISBN 0 7131 5823 9 (cloth)
ISBN 0 7131 5824 7 (paper)

Acknowledgements
The publishers acknowledge permission received from Princeton University Press
to reprint material from *The Machiavellian Moment* by J.G.A. Pocock, © Princeton
University Press 1975; and from Oxford University Press to reprint material from
Democratic Theory by C.B. Macpherson, © Oxford University Press 1973.

Printed in Great Britain by Whitstable Litho Ltd, Whitstable, Kent.

Contents

vi   Preface

2   Introduction
      R. S. Neale

28   **1** The Medieval Social Picture
      H. E. Hallam

50   **2** On the Ruins of Feudalism — Capitalism?
      F. J. West

62   **3** Early Modern Capitalism: the Augustan Perception
      J. G. A. Pocock

84   **4** 'The Bourgeoisie, Historically, Has Played a Most
      Revolutionary Part'
      R. S. Neale

104   **5** Capitalism and the Changing Concept of Property.
      C. B. Macpherson

126   **6** Beyond Bourgeois Individualism: the Contemporary Crisis
      in Law and Legal Ideology
      Eugene Kamenka and Alice Erh-Soon Tay

145   Notes on the Contributors

Preface

Since its formation in 1969, the History of Ideas Unit in the Research School of Social Sciences of the Australian National University from year to year has presented a series of lectures or arranged a weekend seminar on concepts or events that stand out in the history of modern thought, that will help bring together men and women working in different universities and different fields, in many cases in different countries, and make a contribution to the culture and thinking of a wider public. The first such series of lectures, presented as the A.N.U.'s University Lectures for 1970, was published under the title *A World in Revolution?* and is already in its fourth printing. The second set, published by ANU Press as *Paradigm for Revolution? The Paris Commune 1871-1971*, and the third, *Nationalism – the Nature and Evolution of an Idea*, have also had a gratifying response from reviewers and the reading public.

Much of the impetus for the organisation of these lectures and seminars, and much of their success, has stemmed from the presence in the Unit, as Visiting Fellows, of some very distinguished thinkers from overseas – Professor Karl August Wittfogel during the World in Revolution series, Dr Maximilien Rubel for the Paris Commune lectures and Professors Avineri, Mosse and Plamenatz for the Nationalism series. Their considerable contribution to the success of these lectures has been augmented, most significantly, by our being able to draw on the talents and generosity of other departments in our University, of other Universities, and of the wider Australian intellectual community – on Dr Ian Turner, Professor George Rudé and Professor P. H. Partridge for the Revolution lectures, on Professor R.B. Rose, Dr F.B. Smith and Professor Austin Gough for the Commune series, on Professor Wang Gungwu and Professor F.X Martin of University College, Dublin, and La

Trobe University for the Nationalism lectures. One mentions these names, from Australia and from overseas, with gratitude because they have given us the confidence and the intellectual substance with which to embark upon a series that is now, with this book, reaching its fourth volume.

In 1973, when Professor J.G.A. Pocock of Washington University in St Louis, Missouri and Professor C.B. Macpherson of the University of Toronto were working in the Unit, we organised, in place of public lectures, a weekend seminar under the title 'Capitalism — The Emergence of an Idea'. It was meant to explore an idea of overwhelming world-historical importance, enormous complexity and even greater untidiness. We were very lucky indeed, in having — apart from our visitors — Professor H.E. Hallam of the University of Western Australia, Professor R.S. Neale of the University of New England, Dr Francis West of our own University, and Professor G.S. Yule of Ormond College to present papers. Chairmen of the sessions included Professor C.P. Kiernan of Wollongong University, Professor D.M. McCallum of the University of New South Wales, Professor Colin Howard of the University of Melbourne Law School and Dr Robert Banks of the A.N.U. Discussions were opened by Mrs Sybil Jack of Sydney, Dr Alison Patrick of Melbourne and Professor C.M. Williams, Dr R.F. Brissenden and Dr S.J. Stoljar of the Australian National University.

The papers presented here are the outcome of the discussions at that seminar. The idea of capitalism — if there be such an idea at all — proved both fascinating and much too large to be manageable. The participants, quite properly, chose to tackle highlights, nodal points or lines of stress, faults where the whole structure might crumble. But there is little doubt that explicitly or implicitly nearly all our participants had in their sights such a structure — the Marxian conception of capitalism as a total social formation, distinct from feudalism but yet arising out of it, and itself — according to Marx — doomed to give way to a 'higher' mode of social organisation and life. Some of our contributors — Professor Hallam, Professor Pocock and Dr West — are clearly most sceptical of the relevance of many Marxist ways of putting things or of this general Marxist conception of history for the study of either feudalism or capitalism. Some of them are sceptical whether there is such a thing as feuda*lism* or capita*lism* at all. Others — Professor Neale and Professor Macpherson and perhaps Dr Tay and myself — clearly believe that Marx did raise some of the central issues for any general understanding of the dynamic development of Europe and, since then, of the world.

The volume now before the reader, then, does not pretend to be an exhaustive systematic or definitive discussion of the rise, development and possible fall of the complex set of circumstances, ways of working and attitudes that make up capitalism or give rise to its ideology. The volume, rather, is a collection of essays on a theme. These essays make their point in different contexts and in different ways, but always, it seems to me, with insight, originality and a keen sense of what is relevant and what is not relevant in considering great and complex questions of history and of the human condition. The papers are held together not only chronologically, by their moving from a consideration of 'feudalism' to the consideration of aspects of 'capitalism' and of its possible future; they are also held together by the fact that they all contribute in important ways, whether positively or negatively, to considering the truth or falsehood, usefulness or lack of usefulness, of the Marxist account of that movement. In preparing the papers for publication, and adding to them a paper that Dr Tay and I had written for another purpose, I was very fortunate to be able to persuade Professor R.S. Neale to join me as co-editor of the volume and to write for it a substantial introduction. That introduction both presents for us a complex and sophisticated revision and restatement of the Marxist theory of the transition from feudalism to capitalism and brings the remaining papers into relation to each other and to the theme that has emerged from the book. What each contributor would have said to Professor Neale's introduction and to the points raised by his fellow-contributors, the reader is deliberately left to judge for himself. To Professor Neale, to the other contributors and to all the participants in the seminar, to Miss W.G. Gordon, then Secretary of the History of Ideas Unit, and her successor Mrs V. Wetselaar, who have typed and arranged the manuscripts and to Mrs E.Y. Short, Research Assistant in the Unit, who checked the manuscripts and read the proofs, I owe a great debt of gratitude. For the errors that remain I, as the Editor on the spot, take responsibility.

Canberra   *Eugene Kamenka*
March 1974

Introduction

Property, Law, and the Transition from Feudalism to Capitalism

R. S. Neale

I

In the first part of this introduction I will emphasise what seems to me
to be central to each paper and indicate what each has to say about
property and law in relation to the Marxian model. In the second part
of the introduction I will set out in some detail what I believe Marx to
have said about the nature and development of capitalism. This is
because versions of the Marxian model incorporated in the various
papers are but partial versions offered for purposes of debate. Though I
shall also indicate points of emphasis and interpretation which should
help the reader to make his own judgments about the validity of these
various versions of the Marxian model, I will not attempt to assess the
verisimilitude of any of these Marxian models.

In the first paper, Hallam does not address himself directly to any
Marxian concept. He is more concerned to show that the views of Weber
and Tawney about the development of capitalist ideology from the
sixteenth century are false. He argues that capitalistic attitudes and
practices were generated in the agricultural sector of pre-industrial
society in western Europe at least as early as the ninth century. These
capitalistic attitudes, clustering around and developing from notions of
regularity, order, subjection, hard work, the marking of the hours by
clocks, and enumeration and accounting, flourished in Benedictine
monasteries and Carolingian villae. Hallam argues that by the thirteenth
century abbots in eastern England were fully developed economic men
with standards not 'markedly different from the standards of contemporary millionaires'. It is his view that 'by the fifth century materialism
was hard grained within the Christian tradition'. Further, the papacy,
the new western monarchies of the twelfth and thirteenth centuries and
monasticism were the means by which the capitalist mentality took

hard hold upon Europe. Just as the Industrial Revolution was preceded by a great expansion in agricultural output, the ideology of capitalism had rural origins: it sprang 'from the ideas and assumptions of an almost entirely rural society'. Whether or not this notion affects the arguments of Weber and Tawney depends of course on what one considers their arguments to be. Further considerations are whether Hallam's evidence indicates the extent as well as the existence of capitalism and whether capitalism as an objective mode of production was in fact preceded by a significant and widespread development of capitalist ideology in the way he suggests.

West's paper is still on the theme of the nature of feudal society. It also brings us to the matter of law and property and to a direct confrontation with Marx. West outlines the difference between and traces the shift from *beneficium* to *feudum*. *Beneficium* was a form of tenure in which the occupier merely had possession and the grantor retained ownership. However, occupancy carried no labour dues or servile services and rent was moderate or non-existent. The relationship was purely contractual. *Feudum* was a form of tenure in which land was held in return for military service and was sealed by the act of swearing personal fealty. This tied land to man in a bond of vassalage which could be dissolved only by death. During the eighth century this personal relationship began to be combined with the property relationship of the *beneficium*. Although benefice and vassalage were beginning to fuse, the weight given to the two components varied from time to time. By the eleventh century the property element was predominant. The significant point of the argument is that 'feudalism' itself experienced internal change unrelated to any economic development. 'Feudalism' also changed in response to external pressures and developments and these too were of a non-economic kind, particularly in the thirteenth century. In this period the cessation of the barbarian invasions permitted the growth of demesne farming so that erstwhile warriors were able to become landed gentlemen responsive to market forces.

The thrust of West's paper is similar to that of Hallam's. It is that 'feudalism' was not the static unchanging society which Marx, it is alleged, decreed had to be abolished before capitalism could grow. Furthermore, it is argued that the significant changes that did occur within feudalism 'came rather from the feudal lords than from a class challenge to them, certainly in England'. The crucial change, perhaps, was the demise of personal vassalage in the face of the growth of property relations. According to West this is a rejection of the Marxian model which he outlines at the beginning of his paper. In this version of the Marxian model the emergence of capitalism seems to require the destruction or overthrow of feudalism by a bourgeoisie before capitalism could even begin.

With Pocock's paper, we jump some three hundred years from the medieval world which Hallam considered to have been so permeated with capitalism and capitalist ideology to the age of William and Anne in England. According to Pocock this was still a world unknowingly poised for the final economic breakthrough and still a predominantly agrarian society generating an anti-capitalist ideology. Pocock argues that there were still strong vestigial connections between landed property and the bearing of arms. Moreover, virtue was considered to reside in the man of landed property who could bear arms to defend both virtue and property. In West's feudal terminology *beneficium* had yet to supplant *feudum*. As the men of landed property who were also men of virtue looked around them for the revolutionary class against which they measured themselves and which seemed to threaten both their position and beliefs, they did not identify a rationally acquisitive trading or industrial bourgeoisie. The class they saw as the harbinger of the new commercial world of capitalism was drawn from the monied interest and dependents of the crown, such as stockjobbers, rentiers, professional soldiers and placemen. Their property was intangible not real, not property in land but property in rights to revenue from loans and place contingent upon the great growth of government business, war, and the expansion of the national debt. This class, having an interest in and dependence upon governments, sought to advance an alternative system of values in which virtue was regarded as derived from such moveable and intangible property even as credit.

As a defence against the intrusion of the monied interest and newfangled notions about property and credit, men of landed property found themselves asserting radical democratic values. Thus, 'The Augustan version of radical democracy was intended for those, operating whoever they were under an agrarian paradigm, who felt their autonomy and virtue threatened by the manipulative state that went with the credit mechanism'. Democracy came into the world not as the ideology or product of a dynamic bourgeoisie freely acting as producers in a market economy, but riding on the backs of men defending an older agrarian social structure in which landed property alone was considered to confer virtue. Pocock also believes that the story he has to tell is incompatible with conventional Marxism.

In my own paper, I, too, take up and develop the theme of the economically progressive role of men in the agricultural sector empha-

sised by Hallam. Since I write about a period very similar in time to that
covered by Pocock, it might well seem odd that we arrive at dissimilar
interpretations. This is because the dichotomy between landed property
and other forms of property, and between landowners and the monied
interest, isolated by Pocock appears less clear to me. My work in
provincial real estate development and with mortgages and property
law shows that owners of landed property like the Duke of Chandos
and William Pulteney were also stockjobbers, rentiers, placemen, and
soldiers. They were also entrepreneurs. Where they were not all of these
things themselves, their younger sons were and their daughters generally
married other men who were. Thus, while I agree with Pocock that
the trading and manufacturing groups in the late seventeenth and early
eighteenth centuries were not yet the revolutionary bourgeois class of
much of Marxist historiography, I also emphasise the economically
progressive role of landowners. They controlled local government and
parliament and legislated for the financial revolution given so much
prominence by Pocock; they made the financial revolution possible by
legislating for and paying the land tax. Furthermore, they, too, invested
in manufacturing and transport as well as in agriculture. Above all, however, I seek to establish that it was the concern of landowners for their
own interests which led to significant developments in property law. I
argue that law relating to landed property in England became extremely
flexible and functional rather than absolute in the Lockian sense and
that these characteristics of property law were crucial components in
the subsequent development of the industrial sector. I conclude that,
without the long slow transformation of the agricultural sector in the
direction of agrarian capitalism, 'The phenomenon we know as the
Industrial Revolution would have been a non-starter and the question we
are probing would be a non-issue'. Thus to some extent I am in agreement with Hallam and with some of the argument of West. However, I
also make it plain that I do not regard my position as in substantial
conflict with the Marx of *Capital* and the *Grundrisse*.

Macpherson's paper has links with the property aspects of the papers
by West, Pocock and Neale. In the second half of his paper Macpherson
also provides the connection with the 'beyond' in our title, a 'beyond'
in which, as in the past development of western Europe, property and
property rights, and therefore matters of law, will be central.

In the first part of his paper Macpherson draws attention to three
aspects of property in the culture of the west. First, he argues that, by
the time of the development of a full capitalist market society in the
seventeenth century, property had come to mean private property and

the idea of common property had disappeared. The essence of private property was the right to alienate freely and a right to property not conditional on the owner's performance of any social duty. He also points out that a right to property or a right to a share in communal or state property implies the right not be excluded from that right by others. Second, property came to mean absolute property in things themselves rather than claims to revenue from things. Third, property was justified by labour and used as an incentive to labour. In the course of the nineteenth and twentieth centuries each of these aspects of property underwent considerable modification. Thus, as more people have come to depend on various sorts of income guaranteed by states and corporations, the notion that property is a right to a revenue has been revived. Already people think of property as a right to earn an income; men and women in the future can be expected to demand the right not to be excluded from the use or benefit of the accumulated productive resources of the whole society. Consequent on the greatly increased allocative role of the state, Macpherson observes, the function of private property in allocating the use of resources will continue to decline. Further, the use of property to justify labour will cease to be important as industry grows in scale and becomes more automated, so that leisure rather than labour becomes the norm.

In these circumstances Macpherson expects new property rights to emerge. These will be rights to the material means of life, to a free life, and to the fruits of labour. Conversely these rights will means rights not to be excluded from any of these benefits. The only way to establish such rights will be to guarantee to every individual a share in the exercise of political power. Thus property becomes essentially the individual's right to a share in political power.

Macpherson's position is a conventional Marxist philosopher's extension of Marx's future society. It does not deal with the difficult problem of the legal guarantee of such rights at the level of everyday life, guarantees similar in kind to those worked out in the seventeenth and eighteenth centuries to preserve private property.

In their paper, Kamenka and Tay argue that the chief problems facing societies in the 'beyond' will be legal and administrative rather than economico-political ones. It is their view that the abolition of private property has had less effect in removing, or fundamentally altering, the character of social, administrative and legal problems than one might have expected. Their analysis proceeds by isolating three 'ideal' forms of law appropriate to different kinds and concepts of society: *Gemeinschaft, Gesellschaft* and bureaucratic-administrative.

Gemeinschaft law was the product of a society in which the chief concern was with the preservation of the agrarian household as a self-sufficient functioning whole. Its legal norms and forms were the outgrowth of a concept of society as an organic community; people were envisaged as the parts of a tree dependent for very life on the main trunk and roots; the society itself was also static. It was a *Gemeinschaft* conception of law which resulted in the interests and legal personalities of wives, children, and servants being subsumed in that of the head of the family.

Gesellschaft law grew as the economy and man's perception of his place in it changed. It reflected an associative rather than an organic view of society. In this form of law people were regarded primarily as individual atoms or monads moving freely and restlessly, but in an orderly manner. However, they could collide with each other and the function of law was to restore order to these movements by regulating the outcome of collisions. In short, *Gemeinschaft* law was appropriate to groups small enough to be thought of as quasi-individuals; *Gesellschaft* law was appropriate to groups of one, to actual or 'legal' personalities, in a larger self-regulating whole.

The third form of law, bureaucratic-administrative, comes to the fore in technologically advanced societies where the ruling interest or pursued aim appears as 'rational' and to that extent as impersonal and non-human. Its task is to regulate activities involving many groups and interests and large numbers. Thus it 'elevates the socio-technical norm against the private right of the *Gesellschaft* and the traditions and organic living together of the *Gemeinschaft*'.

Kamenka and Tay point out that the traditional socialist critique of *Gesellschaft* law has always vacillated between a yearning for a return to *Gemeinschaft* and adoption of *étatisme* with its emphasis on rational social planning. Thus, the socialist critique reflects the tension between 'two central but contradictory elements in Marxism — technological rationality versus peasant anarchism', and 'conflates *Gemeinschaft* values and bureaucratic-administrative values'. Kamenka and Tay insist upon the need for the clarification of concepts of law and argue that the political shape of the future will depend on the ways in which societies manage to integrate the three ideal forms of law. They make no attempt to predetermine the best mix, though it is probably their view that *Gesellschaft* law should and will continue to play an important role in any mix. Nevertheless, their paper is not a prescription or program of action, but an elaboration of three concepts of law useful to all concerned with resolving the growing problems of the 'beyond'.

All our authors except Hallam and Macpherson make explicit critical comments about one or more aspects of the Marxian model of historical change. Macpherson, however, does seek to expand the Marxist concept of the future society by reference to what he considers to be ongoing developments in the concept of property, while Hallam's paper contains implicit criticism of the Marxian model. All the authors, therefore, locate themselves in the burgeoning and turbulent stream of thought which finds much of its inspiration and orientation in the materialist conception of history. That is the first thread linking these papers together. The nature and content of this concept of history, however, are understood differently by different authors and the point of departure that each author finds in it is determined differently according to the period and problem under review. West questions the suitability of the term 'feudalism' for the economic aspects of medieval society and seeks to show that real 'feudalism' experienced endogenous changes of a legal kind with economic consequences which were contingent upon relationships between the orders of feudal society rather than upon class conflict between feudal lords and an urban bourgeoisie. Hallam, too, is concerned to show the flexibility and change in medieval society. For him economic change was the product of the powers and interest of the church and of its activities in the rural sector. Pocock emphasises that landowners remained a significant political order into the early eighteenth century and seeks to show that radical democracy had its roots in their reaction to their first experience of capitalism. Capitalism impinged on them through activities of the state rather than through the actions of a class of independent bourgeois producers and appeared to threaten their position more by stimulating the growth of arbitrary government and an ideology of dependence than by diffusing ideas of liberty and equality. He concludes that the ideology of liberty and democracy was carried into the eighteenth century on the backs of landowners fighting a rearguard action rather than in the profit-laden pockets of a dynamic and revolutionary bourgeoisie. Neale adopts a somewhat similar position in regard to the development of law in England. In his view law developed in a flexible and functional way as landowners sought to capture more of the revenues of the soil and to found dynasties, rather than through changes induced by responses to the profit expectations of a dynamic and accumulating bourgeoisie, even though the latter did exploit the new forms of law for their own advantage. Macpherson, on the other hand, with the aid of an orthodox Marxist framework, seeks to show how the concept of property changed and is continuing to change as the needs of the bourgeoisie, and latterly the proletariat, have changed and are changing. Kamenka and Tay, critical of that orthodoxy, see a shift in property rights as playing a relatively insignificant part in providing the conditions for the good life. Their paper, by shifting the argument firmly on to questions of law, also throws into sharper focus the second, sometimes hidden, strand linking the other five papers in the collection, the question of law. Kamenka and Tay's concepts of *Gemeinschaft* and *Gesellschaft* law are well worth bearing in mind as the other papers are read.

There are, therefore, two broad issues related to the materialist conception of history touched upon in a variety of ways by all authors. First, there is the question of the nature of the transition from feudalism to capitalism. Second, there is the place of property and law in that transition, as well as in the transition from capitalism to the 'beyond' of our title, a 'beyond' that will have to be built by men conscious of the past forms of society and law and faced with urgent problems arising from the fact of stupendous technological change.

II

It is frequently thought, for example by Hallam and West, that Marx, in writing of the transition from feudalism to capitalism and of the conflict of classes based on property which would generate new societies, envisaged a state of society called feudalism being ruined by a class akin to the fully fledged industrial bourgeoisie of mature capitalism which, in a strange sort of way, has also to be considered as coming into existence *after* the ruin of feudalism. This makes it possible to believe that producing evidence of capitalistic activity in medieval society or showing change within that society to be endogenous indicates that the Marxian categories make nonsense of real history. Similarly the evidence adduced by Pocock and Neale to show significant activity by landowners who carried an agrarian interest and ideology into the modern period on this view is taken as proof that Marx's concept of capitalism does not subsume the real relations of society or represent what really happened in seventeenth- and eighteenth-century England. A parallel phenomenon is the belief of some Marxist historians and thinkers, for example Macpherson, that they have to prove the existence of a buoyant and dominant bourgeois ideology at least by the early eighteenth century.

No doubt there are many reasons why historians believe that these are some of the notions they have to defend or attack to demonstrate their adherence to or rejection of the Marxian schema. One reason is Marx's own propagandist presentation, in a highly abstracted and frequently simplistic manner, of what he perceived to be a historically complex past. For example, in the Preface to *The Critique of Political Economy* Marx wrote, 'In broad outlines Asiatic, ancient, feudal and modern bourgeois modes of production can be designated as progressive epochs in the economic formation of society.'[1] If it is also borne in mind that to these epochs there has to be added a generalised primitive communism with which human society began and the communism with which it will end, it can easily appear that Marx was presenting a stage theory of history comparable to that put forward in outline by W. W. Rostow in *The Stages of Economic Growth.* Thus the Marxian schema could be conceptualised as consisting of six discrete stages through which all societies must inevitably move on their inexorable path to the self-redemption of unalienated man. Such a view too easily discredits Marx as a historian. This section of the introduction, therefore, will attempt to provide an introduction to Marx's own perception of the transition from feudalism to capitalism with the object of building a conceptual framework within which the critiques of Marx contained in this volume may be considered.

Marx can be vindicated in his role as historian in two ways, methodologically and empirically, by examining in some detail the major works in which he presented his historical findings and insights, notably *The German Ideology* (written 1846, first English edition 1938), *The Grundrisse* (written 1857-8, first English editions 1964 and 1973), and *Capital* (written 1865-79, English edition 1887).

First, the question of methodology. For Marx, feudalism and capitalism were, like all his categories, abstractions similar to Weberian ideal types and to Kamenka and Tay's *Gemeinschaft* and *Gesellschaft* forms of law. Their principal defining characteristic was the way in which property was held. They were not discrete stages to be found in the real past, to be rigidly distinguished from each other by their defining characteristic or by any specific overt act or acts of class conflict such as revolution. They were useful analytic concepts but inadequate as descriptions of the real world. Since each ideal type was in process of either becoming or dissolving – the becoming of one necessarily involved the dissolution of the other – there were always elements of the one in the other. Thus the passage from feudalism to capitalism was the history of the last millenium in western Europe, just as the history of the last two hundred years is also the history of the transformation and dissolution of capitalism and the becoming of a new technical-bureaucratic world.

The principal defining characteristic of Marx's feudalism and capita-

[1] K. Marx and F. Engels, *Selected Works*, 3 vols., Moscow, 1969, Vol.1, p.504. Hereafter *Selected Works.*

lism, we have said, was the way in which property was held. The norms
and forms of law and their relation to the development of the economy
lay at the centre of Marx's historical analysis. It is sometimes argued
that Marx solved the problem of the relationship of law to economy in
a simplistic fashion by asserting that law, as a constituent of the ideological superstructure, was causally determined by the economic structure of society. According to this view, forms of law were endogenously
determined within the economic system itself. In one sense this view of
Marx's schema is correct, but only given the existence of a society with
private possession and within an analysis which treats the categories as
ideal types. This is because Marx, like Richard Jones before him,[2] not
only sought to demonstrate the significance of private property for the
economic superiority of western Europe over the rest of the world, but
endeavoured to explain the origin of private property itself in the forms
of society which preceded capitalism. As we follow Marx through his
own researches and reasoning on this question we should be able to
comprehend the distinctiveness of his analysis of the emergence of
western Europe and perceive that his schema is a far more subtle and
complex model of the economic growth of that part of the world than
most historians and many Marxists have been willing to admit. Further,
we should be in a better position to ask whether and in what ways his
analysis of the transition from feudalism to capitalism is affected by
the critiques contained in the papers in this collection.

What follows is neither a history of capitalism nor an appraisal of the
validity of the Marxian model in the light of recent research in economic
history. It is simply an attempt to highlight crucial elements in Marx's
model of the development of western Europe, that is of the transition
from feudalism to capitalism.

In Marx the Asiatic, ancient, and feudal epochs were characterised
by specific forms of economic and social organisation and were alternative historic ways out of a generalised primitive communalism adopted
by various groups of men as they turned to a settled form of agriculture.
As already indicated these epochs were highly abstracted categories
more in the nature of Weberian ideal types than descriptions of the real
world. Each category was identified by the manner in which land was
held and worked, for this has important consequences for the appropriation of the surplus product and further economic and social develop-

[2] Richard Jones, *Literary Remains on Political Economy*, ed. W. Whewell, London, 1859.

ment. In the *Grundrisse*[3] Marx described Asiatic society, comprising
Slavonic and Rumanian communes, Mexico and Peru in their pre-
European period, the early Celts and a few clans in India, as oriental
despotisms characterised by the absence of private property relations,
or by communal property. These societies were largely self-sufficient.
Any surplus product was appropriated by the unity — the community —
and the despot. The individual had no private property in land and was
only a co-possessor of communal property. The constituent communities of Asiatic societies could either vegetate independently alongside
one another or be organised for war, religion, or other communal purposes of the unity. In these societies cities, even though large, were rare,
serving only the purposes of limited external trade, despotic administration, and consumption. The chief characteristic of Asiatic societies was
absence of private property.

In ancient society, on the other hand, some land remained public but
there was also private property in land, and the commune, which was
city-centred, was composed of independent landed proprietors organised
for war against other similar communities. However, private possession
of land derived from membership of the commune. That is membership
of the unity, the city-based commune, was prior to and a condition of
the holding of private property. The purpose of property was to ensure
the proprietor's ability to serve the commune. Thus owners of private
property, as citizens, did not engage in wealth-producing activity for
self-aggrandisement but for communal or unity objectives. Labour was
mainly slave labour. The private proprietor of land was therefore an
urban citizen and 'Urban citizenship resolves itself economically into
the simple form that the agriculturalist [is] a resident of a city'[4] — i.e.
an absentee rather than a resident working proprietor. Slavery remained
the basis of the economic system and a proletariat never achieved an
independent development. This set of conditions made Marx write,
'Rome . . . never became more than a city; its connection with the
provinces was almost exclusively political and could, therefore, easily
be broken again by political events.'[5] The point here was that the city,
which remained an administrative and political centre and the centre of
a robber economy, failed to develop industrially, and failed to establish
complex economic linkages with its agricultural hinterland. Economic

[3] Karl Marx, *Grundrisse*, Pelican Marx Library, London, 1973, pp.471-514.
Hereafter *Grundrisse*.

[4] Ibid., p.484.

[5] Karl Marx, *The German Ideology*, Moscow, 1968, p.34. Hereafter *German
Ideology*.

activity remained tied to nature and the only links between town and country were political, therefore brittle and easily changed by political factors. The defining characteristic of the form of property in ancient society was the subordination of private property to citizenship.

The third form of property was Germanic. In this form no land remained in the possession of the community, unity, or despot. Neither was a member of the commune a mere co-possessor of land at the will of a despot. In Germanic society 'Communal property as such appears only as a communal accessory to the individual tribal seats and the land they appropriate',[6] that is private possession (following conquest) was prior to any communal property which might have been permitted to exist. This flowed from the fact that Germanic society was a dispersed rural-based society in which the commune had more the character of a free association of possessors than in ancient society; thus there was no city-centred commune or unity outside the private possessor with a life and purpose of its own. As Marx put it, 'The commune thus appears as a coming together, not as a being together, as a unification made up of independent subjects, landed proprietors, and not as a unity.'[7] The economic totality was, at bottom, contained in each individual household (*Gemeinschaft*) and the agriculturalist was not an inhabitant of a city, therefore not a member of a state as in ancient society. Instead the larger community was maintained 'by the bond with other such family residences of the same tribe, and by their occasional coming-together to pledge each others' allegiance in war, religion, adjudication etc'.[8] Thus the basis of the commune was a free contractual relationship between private possessors (*Gesellschaft*), but between private possessors as households.

Compared with Locke's account of the origin of private property, which was largely fictional, unhistorical rather than ahistorical, Marx's was grounded in history and could be thought of as rational and scientific. His analysis of Germanic society bears some resemblance to that put forward by Charles Hall,[9] drawing on the work of Dr Gilbert Stewart, in 1805, and by Richard Jones in the early 1830s. It is an argument which asserts the primacy of the socio-political structure of society over the economic and emphasises the crucial role of legal relationships. It might also be thought of as a racialist argument. In any

[6] *Grundrisse*, p.484.

[7] Ibid., p.483.

[8] Ibid., p.484.

[9] Charles Hall, *The Effects of Civilization*, London, 1805.

event, what Marx emphasised was that in all three types of society men were not only bound to nature as agriculturalists but by the socio-political structures of their societies. Only Germanic society contained the possibility of release. It did so by permitting a host of individual landowners to pursue their own economic activities and to appropriate the whole of the product.

Marx's concern with these property relations of his categories arose from his attempt to explain the undeniable fact that capitalism did emerge in western Europe and did blossom in the most unlikely place, England, which was a primary-producing rural backwater as late as the mid-fifteenth century. If embryonic capitalism emerged at all in the ancient world it certainly did not thrive there, and it had neither emerged nor experienced a forced blossoming in Asiatic society by the mid-nineteenth century.

So Marx turned his attention to describing the process whereby the favourable conditions of Germanic society generated further economic change through feudalism to capitalism. In the *German Ideology*, written and published before the *Grundrisse*, he had already emphasised that western European feudalism had its own unique origin specific in time and place as well as in socio-political structure and in legal forms. Displaying his comparative structural approach he wrote,

> If antiquity started out from the *town* and its little territory, the Middle Ages started out from the *country. This different starting point* was determined by the sparseness of the population at that time, which was scattered over a large area and which received no large increase from the conquerors. *In contrast to Greece and Rome, feudal development at the outset,* therefore, extends over much wider territory, prepared by the Roman conquests and the spread of agriculture at first associated with them. The last centuries of the declining Roman Empire and its conquest by the barbarians destroyed a number of productive forces; agriculture had declined, industry had decayed for want of a market, trade had died out or been violently suspended, the rural and urban population had decreased. *From these conditions and the mode of organisation of the conquest determined by them, feudal property developed under the influence of the Germanic military constitution.* [10]

Since Marx also refers to towns, as centres of production and there-fore as capital accumulation, as being created *anew* in the feudal period and not growing as mere extensions of existing administrative and com-merical centres or of the unity-centred cities of ancient society, there

[10] *German Ideology*, p.35. My italics.

can be little doubt that Marx did not envisage feudalism as an outgrowth of ancient society which was basically a unity-centred city society with many cities.

According to Marx the next major characteristic development within feudalism, which itself absorbed Germanic private possession, was the separation of town (manufacture) from country (agriculture). Marx referred to this as the first great division of labour. It had never existed on any substantial scale in Asiatic, ancient or Germanic societies but occurred only within feudalism as a necessary step in economic progress freeing man as agriculturalist from dependence on nature. Paradoxically the separation of town and country began in the countryside. Thus the crucial source of the development of capitalism within feudalism was a dispersed agricultural society blessed with private possession and able to separate itself into town and country. Marx's summation of this notion in the *Grundrisse* is:

> *The Germanic commune is not concentrated in the town;* by means of such a concentration — the town as centre of rural life, residence of the agricultural workers, likewise the centre of warfare — the commune as such would have a merely outward existence, distinct from that of the individual. The history of classical antiquity is the history of cities, but of cities founded on landed property and on agriculture; Asiatic history is a kind of indifferent unity of town and countryside (the really large cities must be regarded here merely as royal camps, as works of artifice erected over the economic construction proper); the Middle Ages (Germanic period) begins with the land as the seat of history, whose further development then moves forward in the contradiction between town and countryside; *the modern [age] is the urbanization of the countryside, not the ruralization of the city as in antiquity.*[11]

In order to comprehend the nature of this process and to understand the significance of the countryside as the place of origin of capitalism it is necessary to give some account of Marx's concepts of mature feudalism and capital.

Marx's mature feudal society rested on the private possession of Germanic society. It was overwhelmingly an agricultural and settled society characterised by a small number of estate or landed properties held by landlords in a hierarchical structure of landownership. The landowners kept armed bodies of retainers which ensured their coercive power over the serfs. Serfs were tied to landed property but had possession of the land. Nevertheless, there were markets and money and towns

[11] *Grundrisse*, p.479. My italics.

were being newly created by the first division of labour, a process completed in Germany by the twelfth century. Consequently serfs moved to the towns and were the making of the towns. In the towns landowner-ship had its counterpart in the shape of corporate property and the organisation of trades, and private property consisted of the labour of the individual with small capital commanding the labour of journeymen. Apart from this first division of labour between town and country there was little division of labour within the towns or within agriculture. Production was mainly for use and there was little specialisation between regions. At the political level there were associations of larger territories into feudal kingdoms with monarchs at their head and associations of towns. But, as Marx was careful to point out, 'Empirical observation must in each separate instance bring out empirically, and without any mystification and speculation, the connection of the social and political structure with production'.[12] Therefore he did not impose an identical political superstructure on the economic structure of the ideal economic type feudalism.

The corollary of private property in land was an obligation imposed on producers to perform some form of service. Under feudalism the direct producer was the serf who had possession if not ownership of the land. The terms of possession varied according to the custom of the manor from 'time immemorial'. According to Marx servile tenure had practically disappeared from England by the end of the fourteenth century. It was replaced by forms of peasant landholding which came very close to freehold, such as copyhold and lifehold. Thus the fifteenth century was the heyday of the English peasantry. The end of the fifteenth century and the early years of the sixteenth were marked by the development of large-scale capitalist agriculture. This happened as commercial production had the effect of concentrating property rights in land in fewer hands and as feudal property became private property. Marx subsumed this long drawn out process in the countryside in the following terms:

> This history of landed property, which would demonstrate the gradual transformation of the feudal landlord into the landowner, of the hereditary, semi-tributary and often unfree tenant for life into the modern farmer, and of the resident serfs, bondsmen and villeins who belonged to the property into agricultural day-labourers, would indeed be the history of the formation of modern capital.[13]

[12] *German Ideology*, p.36.

[13] *Grundrisse*, pp.252-3.

To understand the full import of this proposition of Marx it is
necessary to switch to the end of the process, capitalism. But before
doing so I would like to re-emphasise two characteristics of medieval
society to which Marx himself repeatedly drew attention. The first was
the existence of newly created towns as centres of petty manufacturing,
of non-agricultural production. It is important that these towns be con-
ceptually distinguished from cities like Paris or London as well as from
the cities of Asiatic and ancient societies. Many were really little more
than villages and all were urban islands drawing life from the countryside and giving life back to it. The second was the development of commercial and capitalist agriculture, particularly in England. These two
developments were two sides of the same coin, the division of labour
between town and country, a division which occurred initially and
chronologically *within* the epoch Marx called feudal. The point is that
agrarian capitalism and petty production did not develop after feudalism
— they were integral to it — and feudalism, built on Germanic society
and private possession, was the way out from dependence on nature
which avoided the socio-political constraints of Asiatic and ancient
societies.

It was capital that made capitalism. By capital Marx, like the classical
economists, meant things used to produce more things but, unlike them,
he meant *things so used in certain socio-economic relations*. It was these
relations that made them capital and gave capitalism its specific character. Marx expressed this notion in *Wage Labour and Capital*:

> Capital consists of raw materials, instruments of labour and means of
> subsistence of all kinds, which are utilised in order to produce new
> raw materials, new instruments of labour and new means of sub-
> sistence. All these component parts of capital are creations of labour,
> products of labour, *accumulated labour*. Accumulated labour which
> serves as a means of new production is capital.
> So say the economists.
> What is a Negro slave? A man of the black race. The one explanation
> is as good as the other.
> A Negro is a Negro . . . A cotton-spinning jenny is a machine for
> spinning cotton. It becomes *capital* only in certain relations. Torn
> from these relationships it is no more capital than gold itself is *money*
> or sugar the price of sugar . . . Capital does not consist in accumu-
> lated labour serving living labour as a means for new production. It
> consists in living labour serving accumulated labour as a means for
> maintaining and multiplying the exchange value of the latter.[14]

[14] *Selected Works*, Vol.I, pp.159, 161.

The implication of these paragraphs is that Marx excluded from the concept 'capital' the tools of subsistence agriculturalists and of farmers producing principally for immediate use, as well as the equipment or things which merely facilitated the provision of personal service, and the tools of the petty producer who himself appropriated the whole value of his product. Since the things these people used were not capital, economic systems in which their kind of labouring activities predominated were not capitalist. This notion, that things were only capital when in a market economy they were used in conjunction with wage labour to produce more things not for immediate use but for sale, was a good working hypothesis. It still left open to empirical investigation what to include. But there was more to capital than this. For Marx capital was a polemic sign pointing to much more than things themselves. Capital implied organised production for a market. This in turn required developed monetary and credit systems and a free wage labour force with no ties with the land and no share in the ownership of the means of production. Organised production for the market also meant sustained organisation and manipulation of the resources of nature, including labour, for the purposes of changing the form of those resources in order to produce new products. The essence of capital and capitalism was production, but production for exchange; neither production by itself nor exchange by itself, but both together as the dominant form of economic activity. Therefore, neither self-sufficient peasant groups nor merely trading communities could be thought of as capitalist. In one sense this view boils down to the notion that a spade in the hands of the peasant owner producing for consumption has different socio-economic consequences from a spade placed by its owner in the hands of a wage labourer. The reason for this was that when the wage labourer and the owner of the spade (the capitalist) entered into a contract the exchanges made were not exchanges of equivalents. The capitalist paid the wage labourer a money wage which produced a real wage always less than the value of the wage labourer's contribution to the total product. In short, the wage labourer sold his labour power which produced a value over and above the value he himself received for the production and reproduction of his own labour effort. This surplus labour produced surplus value which was appropriated by the capitalist who used it to acquire more things for the purpose of producing more things — capital. Capital was accumulated labour and, because it was this, it was more than things, however organised. To understand what it really was it is necessary to digress a little.

As a student Marx believed what the enlightenment professed, that man was the measure of all things. Philosophy, he wrote, 'makes no secret of it. Prometheus' confession, "in a word I detest all the Gods", is its own confession, its own slogan against all Gods in heaven and earth who do not recognise man's self-consciousness as the highest divinity.'[15] Subsequently he argued that the essence of man as a species was to be a productive and creative being alone able to make things and men.

He also argued that capitalism alienated man from his essence, and the labour theory of value, summarised briefly in the preceding paragraph, was but an economic expression of this notion. Thus the concept of surplus value embraced the concept of the alienated essence of man although it is worth pointing out that what was appropriated was the product of that essence not the essence itself. Marx expressed the connection between essence, alienation and the exchange of labour on several occasions.

> In exchange for his labour capacity as a fixed, available magnitude, he [the worker] surrenders its creative power, like Esau his birthright for a mess of pottage.[16]

> But the exercise of labour power, labour, is the worker's own life-activity, the manifestation of his own life. And this *life-activity* he sells to another person in order to secure the necessary *means of subsistence* . . . He does not even reckon labour as part of his life, it is rather a sacrifice of his life.[17]

> Selling is the practice of alienation.[18]

In short, labour power had two sides: considered economically, through its ability to generate surplus value it created capital as private property; but surplus value was produced by surplus labour which, considered humanistically by Marx, also appeared as the alienated essence of man. Therefore, in Marx, capital was more than mere property in physical things, or in things disguised in money, or in things disguised in credit. It was also more than what I described at the beginning of this discussion on capital. It was private property in labour — property in the essence

[15] From the preface to Marx's doctoral dissertation, cf. K. Marx and F. Engels, *Werke*, Engänzungsband, Berlin, 1968, p.262.

[16] *Grundrisse*, p.307.

[17] *Selected Works*, Vol.I, p.153.

[18] 'Die Veräuszerung ist die Praxis der Entäuszerung', in 'Zur Judenfrage', K. Marx and F. Engels, *Werke*, Bd 1, Berlin, 1957, p.376. This is translated as 'Objectification is the practice of alienation' in T. B. Bottomore (ed.), *Karl Marx: Early Writings*, London, 1963, p.39, and as 'Selling is the practice of externalization' in L. D. Easton and K. H. Guddat (eds.), *Writings of the Young Marx on Philosophy and Society*, Garden City, N.Y., 1967, p.248.

of man. The principal legal manifestation of this relationship was the development of law relating to wage contracts whereby, as Renner put it, 'Property becomes control over strangers.'[19] Capital, therefore, was alienated labour, labour objectified and reified – a force outside man with economic and legal powers of appropriating more surplus (alienated) labour – a force as hostile as it was necessary to man.

Capital was necessary to man because in pre-capitalist economic systems man was also limited in his ability to realise his creative and therefore his human powers. This was because he applied his labour only to natural objects, that is the land and its products, and as long as man remained little more than a gardener he was bound to remain tied to nature and dominated by it. Thus it was capital and the moment of its creation which provided the initial conditions for man to create himself free from the restraints of nature.

Historically the first step in releasing man's productivity was agriculture. The second, as we have seen, was a society blessed with private possession which became private property which carried with it power to appropriate surplus value. The third was the shattering of man's dependence on nature. Marx called this the greatest division of labour. 'The greatest division of material and mental labour', he wrote, 'is the separation of town and country . . . The separation of town and country can also be understood as the separation of capital and landed property, as the beginning of the existence and development of capital independent of landed property – the beginning of property having its basis only in labour and exchange.'[20] It was the first moment of capital. As we have seen this first great division of labour began *within* feudalism on the basis of the development of property rights in land and the growth of towns anew. This first great division of labour was also primary accumulation. Primary accumulation was also the moment of capital creation. It was not a once and for all occurrence; moments of capital creation recurred throughout history. What did they entail?

Since, at the moment of the creation of capital, there was neither capital nor wage labour, both had to come into existence at once. So there were two components in primary accumulation. One explained the creation of labour, the yeast which started the whole process fermenting, the other the provision of money which, since there was no labour, was not yet capital and only became capital when used to set labour to work in the manner described. Marx's conclusion about the

[19] Karl Renner, *The Institutions of Private Law*, ed. O. Kahn-Freund, London, 1949, p.115.

[20] *German Ideology*, pp.65-6.

generation of these two elements in capital was that 'capital comes into the world soiled with mire from top to toe, and oozing blood from every pore'.[21]

According to Marx, wage labour developed with the expropriation of the peasantry. This began within feudalism as feudal landlords became landowners. It was made possible by the development and clarification of property rights in land, the first division of labour, that is the growth of towns as markets and producing centres, and the flight of serfs. In Germany this early phase was completed by the twelfth century; in England it came later and was particularly intense and widespread in the period 1460-1520, marked by the breakup of the great lordships, enclosure and depopulation of the countryside. It continued with the dissolution of the monasteries, the consolidation of estates and the development of law relating to private property in land at the end of the seventeenth century, and with enclosures in the eighteenth century. In the nineteenth century it continued with the Highland clearances. In Ireland it happened all the time. Collectively these incidents constituted that 'whole series of thefts, outrages, and tribulations that accompanied the forcible expropriation of the people in the period that lasted from the end of the fifteenth century to the end of the eighteenth'.[22] The effect of the appropriation of land by a small minority was to create conditions favourable to the release of labour from agriculture and the creation of a wage labour force footloose with no ties to the land and as Marx put it 'at liberty for the uses of industry'.

The expropriation of the direct producer in the countryside was accompanied in the agricultural sector itself by other consequences of the development of property rights in land already referred to: the development of capitalist agriculture with rentier landlords, capitalist farmers, and wage labourers.

The second aspect of the primary accumulation of capital and the moment of its creation was the provision of money which, for as long as it did not set wage labour to produce for exchange, was not yet capital. It also had unsavoury origins in Spain, Portugal, Holland, France and England, since 'the treasures obtained outside Europe by direct looting, enslavement, and murder, flowed to the motherland in streams, and were there turned into capital'.[23] Hence the importance of the discovery of the new world and the growth of the merchant adventuring activities

---

[21] Karl Marx, *Capital*, Everyman ed., London, 1962, Vol. 2, p. 843.

[22] Ibid., p. 806.

[23] Ibid., p. 835.

of traders. By the end of the seventeenth and the beginning of the eighteenth century these various contributory streams had coalesced in England in the colonial system, the national debt, taxation and modern production. Moreover, 'to some extent [these factors] . . . relied upon the power of the State, upon the concentrated and organised force of society, in order to stimulate the transformation of feudal production into capitalist production, and in order to shorten the period of transition. *Force is the midwife of every old society pregnant with a new one. It is itself an economic power.*'[24] Thus capital, like property itself, depended for its existence on the socio-political structure of society and on the coercive power of the state. However, because of the penetration of capitalism into agriculture and because of the growth of an interest based on money and credit as well as one based on manu-facturing, Marx saw the state in England at the period as a very complex entity. He wrote:

> With few exceptions it is the struggle between 'moneyed interest' and 'landed interest' which fills the century from 1650 to 1750, as the nobility, who lived in the grand style, observed with disgust how the usurers were devouring them, and, with the building up of the modern credit system and the National Debt from the end of the seventeenth century, lording it over them in legislation etc. Already Petty [1662] speaks of the landowners' complaints over the fall in rents in spite of land improvements. He defends the usurer against the landlord, and puts money rent [interest] and land rent on the same footing.[25]

Marx himself regarded the usurer and the monied interest as principal agents in the primary accumulation of capital through the share they took out of the revenues of landowners. However, the monied interest was important mainly at moments of the creation of capital and was characteristic of early capitalism, and in the late seventeenth and early eighteenth centuries industrial and commercial capitalists aligned them-selves behind the landowners against the monied interest; according to Marx they went 'more or less hand in hand with the landowners against this antiquated form of capital'.[26] Therefore, the state which acted as a

[24] Ibid., p.833. My italics.

[25] Karl Marx, *Theories of Surplus Value*, trans. G. A. Bonner and E. Burns, London, [1954], p.30. Cf. Marx to Annenkov, 28 December 1846, K. Marx and F. Engels, *Selected Correspondence*, London, 1956, p.41: 'Hence burst two thunderclaps – the Revolutions of 1640 and 1688. All the old economic forms, the social relations corresponding to them, the political conditions which were the official expression of the old civil society, were destroyed in England.'

[26] *Theories of Surplus Value*, p.30.

commanding midwife to the new capitalist society was not a state representing or reflecting the interests of the big industrial capitalists or bourgeoisie Marx described in the *Communist Manifesto*. The notion that it was not such a state is also supported by Marx's opinion that the industrial capitalists of the Industrial Revolution were still parvenus in the late eighteenth century. Their increase in numbers paralleled the expansion of factory industry and the enlargement of the sphere of fixed or, in Marx's terminology, constant capital. During the period 1650-1750 the state acted more on behalf of the monied interest than any other single interest group.

Earlier I said that Marx saw the usurer as a principal agent in primary accumulation because he abstracted from the revenues of the landlord. Such transfers were crucial in Marx's analysis since, in spite of all I have said about the importance for capitalism of the development of private property in land and of the growth of capitalist agriculture, Marx believed that there had been only limited potential for growth while England remained a predominantly agricultural country however capitalist its development. He noted that the spread of capitalised production in agriculture had been continually interrupted and that the 'peasantry [was] always being reconstituted, although in smaller numbers and invariably under worse conditions'[27] and concluded: 'Not until large-scale industry, based on machinery, comes, does there arise a permanent foundation for capitalist agriculture. Then the enormous majority of the rural population is fully expropriated; and therewith is completed the divorce between agriculture and rural domestic industry.'[28] Only then did the moveable property of capitalism achieve its civilised victory over the landed property of feudalism: This victory cannot be located earlier than the second half of the eighteenth century. Therefore the second aspect of primary accumulation, that is the provision of money as capital, and the first moment of capital which began with the separation of town and country within feudalism and received a powerful stimulus from the opening of the Far East and the new world from the end of the fifteenth century, also took at least three hundred years to complete in England.

Since both aspects of primary accumulation and the first moments of capital were spread over such long periods of time the bourgeoisie was also a long time in developing. 'We see, therefore,' wrote Marx, 'how the modern bourgeoisie is itself the product of a long course of develop-

[27] *Capital*, pp.829-30.
[28] Ibid., p.830.

ment, of a series of revolutions in the modes of production and of exchange.'[29] Nevertheless, it was in the hundred years or so before 1848 that the bourgeoisie played its most revolutionary part. According to Marx it was during the rule of scarcely a hundred years that it 'created more massive and more colossal productive forces than have all preceding generations together'.[30] The key to this development was the expansion of the market and the legal power of private property which permitted the owners of capital to enter into one-sided wage contracts and appropriate surplus labour which was turned into capital which, in its turn, generated further gains in the productivity of labour. So rapid was the rate of accumulation in this period that it is difficult to avoid the conclusion that this short period, less than one hundred years, was the crucial turning point in Marx's model to which all the rest was preliminary, mere primary accumulation. Thus the bourgeois society of the Industrial Revolution was 'like the sorcerer, who is no longer able to control the powers of the nether world whom he has called up by his spells'.[31] Hence came crises, technological innovation, and concentration of capital beyond anything ever experienced before. The pace of development was such that even the political super-structure and the state, which up to 1750 reflected the on-going struggle between the monied and landowning interests, became by 1848 but a committee for managing the common affairs of the whole bourgeoisie. Thus, although Marx was thoroughly aware of the long process involved in creating the conditions for capital the proximate cause of the industrial world he sought to explain was the appropriation of surplus labour and the rapid accumulation of capital from the end of the eighteenth century.

In his analysis of the development of mature capitalism Marx distinguished two elements of surplus labour as sources of increased productivity: absolute surplus labour and relative surplus labour. Absolute surplus labour could be increased by extending the working day or reducing the amount paid in wages. Obviously the possibility of extracting substantial productivity gains from these measures would grow proportionately less the greater the amount of absolute surplus labour already obtained. Absolute surplus labour was faced with diminishing returns. This would mean that growth would slow down almost to zero. Thus absolute surplus labour was important only in the early phases of the accumulation of constant capital. Thereafter it was replaced by

[29] 'Manifesto of the Communist Party', in *Selected Works*, p.110.
[30] Ibid., p.37.
[31] Ibid., p.38.

relative surplus labour as the main source of productivity gains. Relative surplus labour was the product of labour working for the same amount of labour time and doing so with new technology introduced by capitalists in their drive to accumulate and compete. Just as capital was stored up labour, technology was the product of accumulated social knowledge, but private property protected by law still appropriated the whole of its product and determined its distribution. This distribution was unequal and unequal distribution was the cause of recurring crises.

Because technology had come to determine productivity gains Marx also argued that surplus labour had ceased to be the condition of capital accumulation. He wrote:

No longer does the worker insert a modified natural thing [*Natur-gegenstand*] as middle link between the object [*Objekt*] and himself; rather, he inserts the process of nature, transformed into an industrial process, as a means between himself and inorganic nature, mastering it. He steps to the side of the production process instead of being its chief actor. In this transformation, it is neither the direct human labour he himself performs, nor the time during which he works, but rather the appropriation of his own general productive power, his understanding of nature and his mastery over it by virtue of his presence as a social body — it is, in a word, the development of the social individual which appears as the great foundation-stone of production and of wealth. The *theft of alien labour time, on which the present wealth is based,* appears a miserable foundation in face of this new one, created by large-scale industry itself. As soon as labour in the direct form has ceased to be the great well-spring of wealth, labour time ceases and must cease to be its measure, and hence exchange value [must cease to be the measure] of use value. The *surplus labour of the mass* has ceased to be the condition for the development of general wealth . . .[32]

There this summary of the Marxian model of the transition from feudalism to capitalism must end. It would take at least as long again to summarise Marx's account of the evolution of mature capitalism and to discuss his views on crises and the breakdown of çapitalism, impoverishment, the reserve army, class and class consciousness, revolution, and the future society. The papers which discuss the 'beyond' of our title do not discuss these aspects of Marx's 'beyond'. Instead they isolate the notion of property and some concepts of law in the belief that, while there has been much discussion of all the other aspects of the 'beyond', these matters of property and law, which were central to Marx's own analysis of the emergence of capitalism, have largely been ignored in

[32] *Grundrisse*, p.705.

discussions directed at the general reader. While the relevant papers in this collection do not claim to fill that gap, they do provide some stepping stones and the starting point for discussion.

1

The Medieval
Social Picture

H. E. Hallam

In a recent paper[1] the late Professor J. D. Chambers remarks that
Tawney and Weber were wrong in their assumption that the ideas and
attitudes of modern capitalism sprang out of new religious assumptions
which the Reformation and puritanism fostered. Coulton likewise
observes that the attitudes we call puritanism were strongly present in
the minds of the religious as far back as we can go. The aim of this
paper is to show that the medieval view of the developing economy of
the west takes its colour from the assumptions of an agrarian society
which had received strict training from monasticism. I shall deal, not
with the writings of medieval theologians on such subjects as the *justum
pretium*, usury, the sin of avarice, and so forth, subjects which were
well known to early writers on medieval economic history, the pioneers
such as Cunningham and Ashley (whose notions doubtless influenced
Tawney to think that something new came about at the Reformation)
but with what Mumford called the 'idolum' or milieu of ideas and
symbols common to particular groups or societies – the unspoken
assumptions implicit in the way in which men do things rather than the
frothy irrelevancies of intellectuals. It is in this sense that I have used
the phrase 'social picture', as a sort of mundane counterpart to the
world picture of macrocosm and microcosm which Tillyard wrote about
in *The Elizabethan World Picture*.

 Earlier writers on medieval economic history were very interested in
the mercantile aspects of medieval society and tended to forget that
only a tiny proportion of the economy of Europe, even in the fifteenth
century, was other than agrarian. Just as the social and economic changes
we call the Industrial Revolution had, as a necessary prelude, a great

[1] J. D. Chambers, 'The Tawney Tradition', *The Economic History Review*,
second series, 24(3), August 1971, pp.355-69.

growth in the productive capacity of the land, so the attitudes which went with these social and economic changes sprang from the ideas and assumptions of an almost entirely rural society.

European society had, at the beginning of the dark ages, already for several millenia been a society where many, perhaps most, of its members gained their livelihood by agriculture, rather than by hunting, fishing and gathering, or by rudimentary industries. Such early societies differed strikingly in their characteristics from medieval society: the exploitation of the waste lands of northern Europe, away from the Mediterranean world which had hitherto been the main seed-bed of civilisation — this was the economic theme of European history between 600 and 1300. The colonisation of the waste distinguishes the history of western Europe in the middle ages from the history of all preceding epochs in European history and leads into the further exploitation of other parts of the globe after the age of exploration. The white man's last frontier is on the Pilbara and in the Kimberleys.

The century before the uncertain beginning of this process saw the end of classical civilisation in western Europe with the Gothic wars of Justinian and the destruction of the overwhelming majority of the manuscripts of Latin literature known from ancient authors to have existed. Until the 530s the archives of the Caesars — which could have told us something about conditions in the Roman Empire at all periods of its existence — were still intact in the Lateran Palace. Practically nothing has survived from the indefatigable labours of the Roman bureaucrat but a few doubtful remnants, of indefinable authority and in later copies. What remained of western literacy took refuge with Cassiodorus at Squillace or lurked in the Outer Isles of Britain and Ireland, awaiting the coming of the Roman missionaries who rejoined the barbarians of Europe and the heirs of Roman literacy in Northumbria and Ireland. Two generations before St Augustine's mission, St Benedict wrote his Rule: this document is perhaps, after the Vulgate, the most important writing the middle ages was to read.

Regularity, order, subjection and hard work in a community which practised (or was deemed to practise) poverty and stability in an austere way of life were the characteristics of the Benedictine Rule. The monastic life had existed for three centuries in its Christian form when Benedict took it up and St Basil had already formulated a sensible, long-lived Rule which was to do for the Greek church what the Rule of St Benedict did for the Latin church. The way was not new but the Roman method of pursuing it was an influential novelty which revolutionised the life of medieval Europe.

Benedict's very first chapter inveighs against the *girovagi* and other forms of wandering monk whose scandalous behaviour had led to such juicy episodes in the early history of the church as the Latrocinium or Robber Council in 449. *Stabilitas loci* is the cry at all periods in the middle ages of those who would have the monks fulfil the requirements of the Rule they had sworn to observe. The monastery is a self-sufficient island upon which those who had a vocation could take refuge from the sins and troubles of the time, a sort of communal dark ages pattern for the activities of the Economic Man later portrayed by Defoe in *Robinson Crusoe* and in that unread and unreadable nineteenth-century children's classic, *The Swiss Family Robinson*.

The Rule also lays considerable stress upon the need for subordination. The abbot was to be elected and all major decisions were to be taken in chapter, which was to meet daily. The monks were to swear obedience, however, when they had elected the abbot and throughout the proceedings of the monasteries at all times there runs the theme that age and wisdom are to be respected — the theme we find so strongly marked in a work most relevant to the age of youthful obstreperousness, the *Laws* of Plato. Old men were not only to be tolerated, they were to be admired and followed. Decisions were the work of the abbot and the *maior et senior pars* (and the meanings of *senior* and *seigneur* were totally confused by the eighth century). When a man became a monk he put off the Old Adam and entered religion — was converted — as a staid old man. Whatever his age the tonsure was the sign that he had adopted the manners of old age and cast off the lust and vanities of this world.

> In the Benedictine monastery, Plato's condition for the founding of an ideal commonwealth was at last met in actual life: a crisis, an able leader, a good constitution, a just division of labour, and a group of guardians concerned with the eternal verities and reluctant to undertake the task of government.[2]

Mumford's summary is as accurate as it is eloquent, but the Benedictine monastery was something more than the exemplification of Plato's 'idealism'.

The educated classes in the Roman world had not highly esteemed agricultural labour. The nymphs and shepherds who pirouette their way through the pastoral poems of the centuries from Bion and Moschus to Horace and Vergil are a criticism of the labourer's role. It was the invention of agriculture which, in the opinion of poets and historians alike, led to the decline of morals that Livy, Tacitus and others saw as

---

[2] Lewis Mumford, *The Condition of Man*, London, 1944, p.93.

the dominant trait of the society of their times. Slavery, the *latifundia* and the *ergastulum*, and the failure of the Roman world to abolish the more servile forms of labour, the stress upon an idle and bibulous life of amorous fancies which the greatest of the Augustan poets loved, these were not the sort of institutions to make men love the ploughman with his garlic breath. It was the Rule of St Benedict which first taught men that work is their first duty, whether of hand or head:[3]

> Idleness is the enemy of the soul. And therefore, at fixed times, the brothers ought to be occupied in manual labour; and again, at fixed times, in sacred reading . . . If the needs of the place or poverty demand that they labour at the harvest, they shall not grieve at this: for then they are truly monks if they live by the labours of their hands; as did also our fathers and the apostles.

Benedict also laid down certain fixed hours for reading and then added: 'But if any is so negligent or slothful that he lacks the will or the ability to read, let some task within his capacity be given him, that he be not idle.' All was to be done with moderation and common sense.

Perhaps the most famous characteristic of the Benedictine Rule, and most influential, was the division of the day and night by the offices into periods, whether of rest or activity. The whole day was timetabled and this timetabling was the most novel feature of the Rule. Not for Benedict was the slow lapse of hours in which the classical poets wore away the endless leisure of the ancient world.

> Nunc cantu crebro rumpunt arbusta cicadae.
>   nunc vepris in gelida sede lacerta latet.
> si sapis, aestivo recubans te prolue vitro,
>   seu vis crystalli ferre novos calices.
> heia age pampinea fessus requiesce sub umbra
>   et gravidum roseo necte caput strophio;
> per morsum tenerae decerpens ora puellae.

> Cicadae out in the trees are shrilling, ear-splitting,
> The very lizard is hiding for coolness under his hedge.
> If you have sense you'll lie still and drench yourself from your
>   wine cup,
> Or maybe you prefer the look of your wine in crystal?
> Heigh ho, but it's good to lie here under the vines,
> And bind on your heavy head a garland of roses,
> And reap the scarlet lips of a pretty girl.[4]

[3] Quotations from the Rule of St Benedict are taken from *Documents of the Christian Church*, ed. H. Bettenson, Oxford, 1943, pp.161-79.

[4] Helen Waddell, *Medieval Latin Lyrics*, London, 1933, p.5.

The time and place for everything was laid down in the Benedictine Rule and 'everything' certainly did not include the delights eloquently depicted in the *Copa Surisca*. Baths were to be offered to the sick as often as necessary; to the healthy, and especially to youths, more rarely. According to the *Regularis Concordia*, the monks were to bathe only on Holy Saturday and so terrible was the experience that the old were to encourage the young by words and example to submit themselves to the proof of it. Wine the monks were to have at the rate of a pint a day — with some hesitation for, as Benedict observes:

> We read that wine is not suitable for monks at all. But because, in our day, it is not possible to persuade the monks of this, let us agree at least to the fact that we should not drink to excess, but sparingly. For wine can make even the wise to go astray.

All was to be in due order and sequence.

In the Benedictine monastery the middle ages discovered that time has dimensions which can be measured and treated as if it were a substance. You could use time, spare time, waste time, save time, keep time and allocate it to various needs. Future centuries would also gain time, buy time, make time, work time, kill time, and, if they were criminally inclined, do time. The Benedictine attitude to time created the need for the monastery to know the correct time and to be able to measure its lapse. At first it was sufficient to have in the monastery at least one brother who was skilled in astronomy and who could wake the others to say the night offices. As services became more numerous and complex the mechanical clock came into existence.

Of all the medieval inventions which both express and influence society's attitude to and view of itself the clock is the most significant. The ancient world had known water clocks and this was probably the type Gerbert possessed towards the end of the tenth century. The mechanical clock does not certainly appear until much later and cannot definitely be proved to have begun in the monastery. At least one fifteenth-century monastic alarm clock is known from Italy and the name 'cloister-ring' sometimes applied to the inner ring on early clocks may denote the origin of the mechanical clock.

The earliest authentic examples of mechanical clocks are all town or church clocks. Men of talent were already preoccupied with the problem of devising a mechanical clock in the 1260s. In 1269 a Picard military engineer, Peter of Maricourt, thought that a sphere of magnetic iron, mounted without friction parallel to the axis of the earth, would rotate once daily in sympathy with the heavenly spheres. In 1271 Robert the

Englishman was talking about plans for a weight-driven clock but could not solve the problem of the escapement. At about the same time, at the court of Alfonso the Wise of Castile, Rabbi Isaac ben Sid of Toledo described and drew a weight-driven clock with a brake which consisted of an internally compartmented drum containing mercury flowing through small holes from section to section. By the 1330s the verge and wheel escapements had come into existence, and mechanical tower clocks are known from about this period. There was one at St Eustorgio in Milan in 1309, at Beauvais cathedral before 1324, at St Gothard in Milan in 1335 (this clock struck the twenty-four hours of the day), at Padua in 1344, Bologna in 1356 and Ferrara in 1362. From Italy the mechanical clock spread to France and England. Charles V installed a clock that struck the hours on one of the towers of his palace, so that every citizen might know the time whether the sun shone or not. Around 1345 the division of hours into sixty minutes and minutes into sixty seconds became common and the old custom of dividing both day and night each into twelve different and changing hours began to come to an end. The rationalisation of time had come. In England the earliest known mechanical clocks, which still exist, are at Salisbury and Wells and date from the first half of the fourteenth century. Another early clock was at Dover Castle and is now in the Victoria and Albert Museum.

Yet the spirit of the clock is wholly Benedictine. Its coming taught men that time is something independent of human events and its measurement of time — its actual production of hours, minutes, and seconds — is a very important aspect of the medieval recognition of the significance of numbers. For many generations the clock was the most familiar true machine the ordinary man knew and it is still the most common machine in the world. Its mechanical development for a long time kept ahead of the development of other machines in accuracy of workmanship and ingenuity and set a standard for the rest. It was the perfect automatic, regular, and independent mechanism. Through its medium punctuality came into the world and by the eighteenth century men could say 'time is money'. 'Regular as clockwork' became such an ideal that by the nineteenth century some westerners wanted themselves to become clocks. Benedictine practicality, regularity and moderation the saint regarded as 'instruments of virtue for well-living and obedient monks'.

> We blush with shame for the idle, and the evil-living and the negligent. Thou that hastenest to the heavenly country, perform with Christ's aid this Rule which is written down as the least of beginnings: and then at length, under God's protection, thou wilt come to the greater

things that we have mentioned; to the heights of learning and virtue.

The irony of history is that the very nature of Benedictinism taught men to substitute measurement and time for the limitless expanses of eternity.

Benedictine self-sufficiency fitted well the agrarian economy of the dark ages. Already in the Rule St Benedict had written:

> A monastery should, if possible, be so arranged that everything necessary — that is, water, a mill, a garden, a bakery — may be available, and different trades be carried on, within the monastery; so that there shall be no need for the monks to wander about outside. For this is not at all good for their souls.

By the time of Charlemagne the *polyptiques* show the consequences of this policy in the need which the monasteries felt to account for and regulate their possessions.

The first period of energetic and effective accountancy is the work, in the first place, of the papacy rather than the Benedictine order, but the Benedictines took over the practice and handed it on to the Frankish Empire of Charlemagne. The patrimony of St Peter — the estates of the church of Rome — had been very large even in the fifth century and as far back as the days of Pope Gelasius, in 433, the papacy had looked after its affairs by drawing up *polyptiques*. These documents were statements of receipts and expenses and out of them grew the elaborate accounting system which existed in the days of Pope Gregory the Great. When Gregory became pope in 590 the depredations of the Lombards which followed upon the disastrous Gothic wars of Justinian had left the estates of the church in considerable disarray and the peasantry were subjected to many illegal depredations on the part of the church's lessees. Gregory set out to rectify matters and his own training was such that he became the main avenue by which Roman traditions of good management spread into the medieval church, and so into medieval society. To later generations Gregory was known above all as the great business pope who practised what was sometimes known as economy, or good management.

The esteem in which his successors held him is responsible for the survival of an important part of Gregory's archives in the shape of excerpts from the original letter books in which he kept copies of his instructions to (among others) his administrative officials. In all there are 848 letters and from these the historian can reconstruct a good deal of the administrative method of the papacy about the year 600. The estates were divided into groups, each of which was a *patrimonium* and had its own particular *polyptique*. Receipts and disbursements were all reported to Rome and Gregory issued instructions and advice by letter to his officials. Perhaps the most important estates were in Sicily and, after July 592, these were divided into two separate patrimonies based respectively upon Palermo and Syracuse. There were also patrimonies on the mainland of Italy in Bruttium, Lucania, Calabria (especially at Gallipoli), Campania, Samnium, Sabine (especially at Nursia and Carsolio), along the Appian Way, and, suffering interference from the Lombards, in Tuscany, Istria, Liguria and the Cottian Alps. At Ravenna the church of Rome had a patrimony quite separate from that of the church of Ravenna. There were other estates in Sardinia and Corsica, in Dalmatia and Illyria, at Germanicia in Africa, and in parts of southern Gaul. The estates of the church of Rome were therefore extremely widespread and a quite elaborate organisation was necessary to make sure that the revenues, much of which Gregory devoted to charity, flowed properly to the centre. Each patrimony had a rector, usually a deacon or sub-deacon, whom the pope appointed to the office and who was responsible for the moneys received from the estates. The rector did not farm the estates directly himself: they were let out on lease to *conductores,* who could be freemen, freedmen, or slaves, either on short terms or on terms which could extend to three lives. The tendency was to change the *conductores* fairly frequently so that a new *conductor* could pay a new *libellaticum.* The leases used the old name of *emphy-teusis*, which implies that the lessee had the duty to clear and improve the land and make greater profits from it.

Charlemagne followed the example of St Gregory. The *Capitulare de villis,* probably written sometime before 800, is remarkably rich in detail and reflects the great king's passion for statistics and his immense power of meticulous administration. The Carolingian *villa* was a hive of industry. In the centre of the estate was the lord's house where Charles lodged when visiting his *villa.* The outbuildings were numerous; the capitulary lists the furniture kept in each repository; there were kitchens, bakeries, wine-presses, several cowsheds, stables, byres, sheepfolds, pigsties, a hayloft, and one or more watermills. The enclosure also contained a courtyard and a fishpond and close at hand was a church. In a separate quarter, surrounded by hedges and shut in by solid gates, were the women's lodgings, where they wove linen, made clothes, combed wool and dyed cloth with woad, madder and vermilion. The *villa* also made footwear and shields for the army, and there were turners, joiners and cabinetmakers, makers of carts and litters, forges for weaponmakers

and workshops for goldsmiths. Nonetheless the *villa* was primarily a
farm for growing corn. The mayors, under the direction of the *judex*,
supervised sowing, ploughing and harvesting, dressing vines and making
wine. The writer laid down that winemaking was to be clean and wholesome and that nobody should presume to press the vintage with his
feet. Sound barrels bound with iron hoops were to be used for storing
the wine and leather bottles were to be avoided. Charlemagne drank
great quantities of ale, but the capitulary also specifies mulberry wine,
cider and mead. Water was strictly for washing.

The king gave particular attention to stock rearing. There were
apparently at all the *villae* studs where mares and stallions were kept. The
bailiffs were not to slaughter too many oxen and lame animals were
to be kept for meat, which had to be wholesome and free from infec-
tion. For ploughing, to spare the king's own cattle, the bailiffs were to
use his serfs' cows, but two fat oxen from the domains were to be
brought to his palace each year. Except on fast days, Charlemagne's
kitchens cooked with fat, and he also ate bacon, smoked meat and
sausages. On the three weekly fast days and in Lent there were cheese,
fish and vegetables.

The king even regulated in many provisos sheep, goats, geese,
chickens, eggs, fish from the stewponds, bees, and distributions of wax
and soap. Every year at Christmas the bailiffs were to bring him clear
and accurate accounts of all goods and all money income from his
domains. This does not mean that Charlemagne, any more than the
businesslike churchmen of later centuries, eschewed the luxurious
inessential. He bred fancy birds, such as turtle doves, pheasants, and
peacocks. Even so, the strong strain of thrift is there — worthy of a
Victorian capitalist — and is best illustrated in the last section of the
survey of Asnapium, which is apparently an example of an inventory
drawn up in accordance with the king's instructions:

> The garden herbs which we found were lily, putchuck, mint, parsley,
> rue, celery, libesticum, sage, savory, juniper, leeks, garlic, tansy, wild
> mint, coriander, scullions, onions, cabbage, kohl-rabi, betony. Trees:
> pears, apples, medlars, peaches, filberts, walnuts, mulberries, quinces.

It would be easy to claim that Charlemagne's organisation of his own
estates was peculiar to a man of outstanding administrative capacity,
but he had excellent ecclesiastical advisers, who, following the ancient
traditions of Roman administration, organised their own estates very
carefully. Both Pepin the Short and Charlemagne himself had ordered
their vassals, lay and ecclesiastical, to draw up inventories of their

properties, but the great abbeys probably anticipated their commands by making *polyptiques*. The most famous of these and the most nearly complete is that of the abbey of Saint-Germain-des-Prés in Paris, called, after its abbot, the *Polyptique d'Irminon*. This famous document dates back to the time of Charlemagne and is the most detailed and most accurate of the *polyptiques*. It is a triumph of organisation carried out by a churchman with an outstanding gift for business, who developed agricultural production by using to the best possible advantage the labour force which lay at hand. The inventories of twenty-four domains have come down to us, all except five of them in the suburban belt which surrounds Paris, between Mantes in the west and Chateau-Thierry in the east. They contain particulars of each domain right down to the last egg.

Each 'brief' or chapter is devoted to a *villa* and all are modelled on the same plan. There is first a short paragraph which deals with the demesne *(mansus dominicatus, terra dominicata)* which the tenants of the *mansi* cultivated for the lord. The exact area is described and each brief indicates the quantity of grain to be sown in each field, the number of hogsheads of wine to be produced in the vineyards, the cartloads of hay to be expected from the demesne meadows and the number of pigs to be fattened in the woods.

Then follows the description of the tenants' *mansi*, the enumeration of their dues and labour services, the names of all the tenants and a census of all the households with the number of children in each. The document is highly coherent, has held the attention of scholars for over a century by its fullness and is the perfect exemplar of monastic powers of organisation and industry.

Indeed the early Benedictine monasteries were in charge of estates, each of which became a kind of factory, as did the monastery itself. This was necessarily so, for every religious foundation of any size in the eighth and ninth centuries had to produce corn, wine, hay, textiles, honey, wax, chickens, eggs and so forth on a large scale. The Bavarian monastery of Staffelsee had two dozen serf women at work in a *gynaecea* in the early ninth century. A sketch plan of the monastery of St Gall and the outbuildings grouped around it at this time shews a handicraft house with workrooms and sleeping quarters for tanners, shoemakers, saddlers, goldsmiths, blacksmiths, swordsmiths, shieldmakers, wood-workers, and fullers. Next the brewery was a coopers' shop. The monks of St Gall met all their industrial needs by imposing a rational and disciplined division of labour on their work which would have won the heart of Adam Smith.

After about 900 there was a lapse in the practice of keeping exact accounts of estates which were, perhaps for the most part, no longer directly in the lord's hands. The creation of the Domesday Book by William the Conqueror acted as a great stimulus in England to the keeping of a more systematic check upon production and the example of the papacy, which from 1046 onwards began increasingly to build up an elaborate bureaucracy, and the experience of the Norman kingdom of Sicily added further to the desire to revive old methods. In England from the time of Henry I onwards, and perhaps earlier, great churchmen were lending their knowledge and administrative talent to the devising of western Europe's most advanced accounting system — that of the Exchequer.

The *Dialogus de Scaccario* of Richard son of Nigel illustrates the mental attitudes of the clerical bureaucracy — his father, Nigel, Bishop of Ely, had been Treasurer to Henry I, and Nigel's uncle, Roger le Poer, Chancellor, Bishop of Salisbury, and afterwards Justiciar of Henry I. This clerical family was much concerned with the development and efficient running of the English Treasury and Exchequer. The *Dialogus* may have been an official manual issued under the authority of Henry II; already a civil service tradition had developed by 1174-83. The treatise is severely practical and the author a conservative, illogical and sometimes passionate defender of things as they are. He shews a combination of respect for official tradition with a zeal for the public interest which make him a model civil servant. His power of compromise is as remarkable as his fondness for figures and his ability to explain complex matters clearly. His respect for money is tempered by his religion.

> We are, of course, aware that kingdoms are governed and laws maintained primarily by prudence, fortitude, temperance and justice, and the other virtues, for which reason the rulers of the world must practise them with all their might. But there are occasions on which sound and wise schemes take effect earlier through the agency of money, and apparent difficulties are smoothed away by it, as though by skilful negotiation. Money is no less indispensable in peace than in war. In war it is lavished on fortifying castles, paying soldiers' wages and innumerable other expenses, determined by the character of the persons paid, for the defence of the realm; in peace, though arms are laid down, noble churches are built by devout princes, Christ is fed and clothed in the persons of the poor, and by practising the other works of mercy mammon is distributed.[5]

[5] *Dialogus de Scaccario*, trans. Charles Johnson, Edinburgh, 1950.

A Victorian churchman might have uttered similar sentiments.

By the twelfth century counting money had become a respectable occupation for abbots, bishops, popes and kings. Religion and the prejudices of feudalism which laid stress on otherworldly or more honourable considerations still tempered what was to become the ruling passion of the modern capitalist and bureaucrat, and already the lineaments of both these modern classes are visible in the able churchmen of the day. Many historians, when studying the later middle ages, have looked at merchants, industrialists and bankers to see the origins of modern capitalist attitudes. Industry and banking were not responsible for much of the generation of liquid capital, which (amongst other factors) was necessary for the take-off into the Industrial Revolution which began in the sixteenth century. It is to agriculture that we look for both the growth of capital and the generation of the right attitudes. The medieval social picture — its view of its own developing economy — is not only ecclesiastical and specifically monastic, it is also rural.

The eleventh and much of the twelfth century were periods in which great landowners let out most of their estates to lessees or tenants-at-will but in the second half of the twelfth century the new surge of population growth led to a rise in the demand for food and in the supply of labour necessary to produce that food. The thirteenth century was therefore the golden age of the great landowner who farmed his own properties through bailiffs. The new spell of monastic interest in accounting came, in England, at a time when the English state was organising its Exchequer afresh and the two movements towards an interest in accounting and mensuration lent each other aid.

A good example of monastic methods, stimulated by royal interest in the estates in a period when the abbacy was vacant, is the *Black Book of Peterborough* 1125-8. Of the manor of Kettering in Northamptonshire it says:

> In Kettering are 10 hides at the King's geld. And of those 10 hides 40 villeins hold 40 rods of land. And those men plough at the lord's work for each rod at the summer sowing 4 acres. And besides this, in winter they find ploughs 3 times at the lord's work, and 3 times at the summer sowing, and once in summer. And those men have 22 ploughs with which they work. And all those men work 3 days in the week. And besides this they render each year from each rod of custom 2s. 1½d. And all the men render 50 hens, and 640 eggs. And besides this Aegelric holds 13 acres, and from it renders 16 pence with 2 acres of meadow. And there is a mill with a miller, and it renders 20 shillings. And 8 cotsetes, each of five acres, and they work once a week, and make malt twice a year. And each of them gives 1

penny for a goat; and if he has a wife, she gives a halfpenny. And
there is 1 shepherd, and 1 swineherd, who holds 8 acres. And in the
demesne of the court are 4 ploughs of 32 oxen, and 12 cows, with
10 calves, and 2 animals who do not plough, and 3 pig-styes, and
300 sheep, and 50 pigs, and as much additional meadow as is worth
16 shillings. And the church of that town to the altar of the Abbot
of Peterborough. To the charity of saint Peter 4 rams and 2 cows or
5 shillings.[6]

Already the interest in numbers is sufficient to satisfy even a modern
North American, who cannot open his mouth without telling you a
number.

Later surveys and extents are much more detailed than this example.
They usually give the name of every tenant and his condition and often
the names and holdings of sub-tenants and parceners. There are usually
elaborate statements of customs, works and rents as early as the 1227
surveys of the estates of the Bishop of Ely or the Domesday of St Paul's
in 1222. A few eastern England surveys, such as the great surveys of the
manors of Spalding Priory made in 1259-60 or some of the later surveys
of the Cathedral Priory of Norwich name and describe very carefully
each strip of land held by every tenant. In eastern England measure-
ments of *terra mensurata* can be very exact, not just to the nearest half
perch, but frequently to the nearest foot and sometimes to the nearest
6 inches. The survey of Martham made in 1292 lists 935 different people
who occupied 2021 separately described strips in an area of 830 acres
2 roods. The practice of partible inheritance and a rapid population
growth were responsible for the shape of Martham in 1292 but the
Cathedral Priory of Norwich kept careful check of what was happening.
Originally there had been about twenty-two and a quarter twelve-acre
eriungs or standard holdings which in the course of the thirteenth
century had become greatly sub-divided. An example of the care which
the priory had to exercise will be the Hil holding. Early in the thirteenth
century Roger de Hil held ten acres of *mulelond*. In 1292 eleven
tenants, three of them his descendants, held the same land as follows:

Robert de Hil, senior	1 acre 1 rood 23 perches 6 feet
John de Hil	1 acre 1 rood 23 perches 6 feet
Robert de Hil	1 acre 1 rood 33 perches 6 feet
Adam Harding	10 perches
Eustace Stannard	2 acres 1 rood
John Attewelle	3 acres

[6] Translated from *Chronicon Petroburgense*, ed. Thomas Stapleton, Camden
Society 47, 1849, pp.157-8.

Beatrix Alexander	2 acres
Geoffrey de Sco	2 roods 10 perches
Robert de Sco	2 roods 10 perches
Simon son of William Sco	2 roods 10 perches
James son of William Sco	2 roods 10 perches

The preoccupation with numbers had gone a very long way by the end of the thirteenth century.

Historians have known for a good number of years that, in spite of lordly conventions about money grubbing, great landlords, ecclesiastical, royal and noble, practised large-scale farming for wheat and wool in the Lowlands, and for cattle, cheese and horses in the Highlands in the thirteenth century, but it is only in the monastic chronicles that one perceives the approval, even enthusiasm, with which the monks regarded these worldly activities. The good abbot was a building and farming abbot. To illustrate this point I shall summarise briefly what the Peterborough chronicler Walter of Whittlesey, probably writing soon after 1223, has to say about the abbacy of his contemporary Godfrey of Crowland. The Peterborough estates were extensive so I shall refer mainly to the manors of Boroughbury, Eyebury, Fiskerton and Thurlby.

Abbot Godfrey of Crowland had probably had long training as a man of affairs, for when elected to the abbacy in 1299 he had been cellarer of the abbey, an office which brought with it a multitude of cares. After his death in September 1321 the survey which the royal escheators made shewed that the four manors mentioned were worth £165 12s. 7d. His energy was the more remarkable since the period of his abbacy is supposed to have been a time of great difficulty and decline and indeed the anonymous continuator of Walter of Whittlesey, writing about 1338, does say that in 1321 there had been great scarcity of corn for six years because of the sterility of the earth and the floods of water and that in 1321-2 the stocks of corn had scarcely been sufficient to last the abbey until the Feast of the Purification.

In 1299 Abbot Godfrey completed at Eyebury a very beautiful hall which his predecessor Abbot William of Woodford (1295-9) had begun, at a cost of £6 16s. 11½d., and he enclosed for his deer land which had formerly been pasture.

In 1300 at Boroughbury he made a new dovecote — cost 79s. 9½d. and a new pool with a dyke planted with willows on one side outside the gate on the western side — cost £21; at Eyebury a new building, bakery and dairy — cost £6 9s. 1½d.; at Rumpele near Eyebury a new rabbit warren — cost 9s. 7d. — and a new garden suitably laid out with apple and pear and other trees — cost 24s. 6d. He also built a new cow-

shed with its enclosures next Oxney with entrance and exit by a bridge
to Borough Fen — cost 100s.

In 1301 at Eyebury he made a new windmill because the old one had
been burnt — cost £6 6s. 4¾d.; at Fiskerton, a new stable — cost
£8 14s. 4½d. and a building to receive ships at the gate of Bolehithe. He
lengthened the chancel at Oxney at a cost of £12 4s. and glazed three
windows in the chapel — cost £10. He also made a beautiful herb
garden next the garden Dereby, which he surrounded with double pools,
bridges, pear trees and most delicate herbs at a cost of £25 and he
acquired an alder grove between the herb garden and the river Nene.

In 1302 at Eyebury he built a stable — cost 7s. 5d. — and made a new
dyke lined with willows between Tanholt and the new meadow — cost
£6 19s. 8d. At Fiskerton he made a willow-lined dyke between the park
close and the fen at a cost of 20s. 3d.

In 1303 at Eyebury he built a new dovecote at a cost of 47s. 2d.
and began the manor of Northolm. Here there had never been a manor
before; it had lain as pasture. He also enclosed the meadow of
Cranemore, some 200 acres and more, and out of arable land on the
eastern side of Cranemore planted a wood and called it Childholm.
Three other holmes in the fen he surrounded with a dyke lined with
willows, ashes and oaks, made a new dyke from the river Nene to the
manor of Northolm and another dyke between the Reach and the fen at
a total cost of £31 2s. 9½d. He also bought a messuage, a toft, 74 acres
of land, and 4 acres of meadow with appurtenances in the towns of
Peterborough, Walton, Dogsthorpe, Carton, Newark, Thorpe and Eye
for £60, including gifts and other courtesies. This was called the fee of
Gymicius.

In 1304 he made a causeway below Borough Park with a willow-lined
dyke, completed the manor of Northolm at a cost of £38 0s. 3d. and
planted a wood next the manor. At Fiskerton he made another new
dovecote — cost 36s.

In 1305 at Boroughbury he enclosed a long meadow and made a
willow-lined dyke at a cost of 20s. He built and dedicated a new chapel
at Northolm for £8 16s. 9d. and obtained from the king a charter to
hold a fair there for two days each year and a Thursday market each
week.

In 1306 he enclosed Borough Park for £4 15s. and made a willow-
lined dyke between Thorpe Fen and the Dam for 20s.

In 1307 at Peterborough he made a new bridge over the Nene, which
was destroyed by ice the following winter, for £14 8s. and next Thorpe
Fen a willow-lined dyke for 35s. 5d; at Eye half a great new barn for

£45 19s. 11d; at Thurlby a new wall round the manor for 20s. and a new wall between the herb garden and the Derebyyerd. In 1308 at Thorpe he rebuilt the ruined dovecote for 46s. 0¼d. At Peterborough he built another bridge across the Nene, higher and stronger than the first, at a cost of £18 5s. He also gave the abbey the newly acquired manor of Lullington and the 74 acres of arable and 4 acres of meadow of the fee of Gymicius, with 18 pence rent, and all the meadow with the new causeway between Borough Fen and Oxney Lode, which the abbot had likewise acquired, to support a priest in Northolm chapel.

In 1309 at Boroughbury he made a new hall for the servants for £4 0s. 6d. and began a new pool on the east side of the way, with a watermill, and a wall on the west side of the pool and surrounded the pool with a willow-lined dyke at a cost of £62 6s. 7d. At Eye he finished the other half of the barn, strong and great, at a cost of £50 9s.6d. This barn, after his death, was completely burnt down as a result of putting wet, green hay in it. He also enlarged the garden at Eye, enclosed it with a new wall and made four very beautiful pools in it, at a cost of £18 2s. 9d. He also made a new horsepond between the mill and the fen.

In 1310 at Eye he built a new chamber at the western head of the hall, covered with lead, with two new gates to the barn, at a cost of £82 0s. 1½d., grubbed out and made a new orchard within the circuit of the new wall, and planted it with different fruit trees, with hedges and dykes around it, at a cost of 44s.

In 1311 at Eye he began a new chamber with a new pantry cellar at the entrance to the hall, with a long privy, both for that and the old chamber; also a new kitchen with an enclosure between the hall and the kitchen. Next Oxney he rebuilt the cowshed previously burnt down. All these cost £42 4s. 7d.

In 1314 at Eye he built a new brewhouse and a new henhouse.

In 1316 at Boroughbury he built a new windmill next Woddhythe, standing near the water, the bank of which he completed with stone in the shape of a porch, at a cost of £4 19s. At Northolm he made a new building and chamber with a rabbit warren at a cost of 40s.

Through these words there glows a sort of pride and satisfaction in the work. The manors named were all near Peterborough and had to be comfortable, but the amount of money spent is enormous. A great lord like the Abbot of Peterborough was just as ostentatious, as likely to engage in conspicuous consumption, as a sixteenth- or nineteenth-century capitalist. His standards do not seem to have been markedly different from the standards of contemporary millionaires and would not have pleased St Benedict. Yet they grew from the observation of the Rule. The interest of medieval churchmen in making money is becoming ever clearer as research proceeds. Jocelyn of Brakelond's account of the life of Abbot Sampson is a classical text here. The proprieties had to be kept where profit-making was concerned, particularly when it was usurious profit-making, but the attitudes and practices of the Benedictine and other abbeys were much more like our own than the nineteenth century dared to think. Take, for example, the business of monastic endowment. Charter form dictates that transfers of property should take the form of a grant, and early transfers, given *in pura libera et perpetua elemosina* were perhaps usually just that, but by the end of the twelfth century in England the form of a grant very often hid the fact that the transfer was in reality a sale or a mortgage. Even when the transfer really was a gift the charter often specified a rent, so that the grant was not a true grant in frankalmoign. Even more interesting are the grants which contained a statement that the grantee had paid a consideration for the transaction, which is in truth the purchase price. Examples of this sort of transaction are very numerous. A simple one is the grant made in 1256-62 to the Prior of Bilsington, Kent, by William son of John of Bilsington of all the land with its appurtenance which he had inherited from his mother Alice in Stephenesfeld at a rent of one *summus* of wheat as *forgabulum*. For the gift the prior and canons gave him 15 shillings and a house with 2 acres of land. Exchanges were also very frequent and enabled lords to build up holdings more conveniently distributed. Even more indicative of the sentiments of monasteries about profit making are the grants in which there is some reference to the economic circumstances of the grantor. Sometimes the charter contains a phrase which indicates that the grantee has made a sum of money available to pay the grantor's debts — such as *in magna necessitate mea* or *in magna paupertate mea*, and there are some charters which say that the money is to pay off a debt owed to the Jews. These latter are found only before Edward I's expulsion of the Jews in 1290. Occasionally reference is made to the need of money to go on crusade. There seems little doubt that until well into the fourteenth century, and sometimes much later, monasteries were buying up properties from impoverished owners or advancing money on the strict understanding that it would not be repaid and that the land granted would become the permanent property of the grantee. All that we know about monastic finances suggests that they were particularly sensitive to the trends of the land market and to the prices of commodities and that they changed their policies to suit the times. In some abbeys and bishoprics there were competent heads and ecclesiastics tended, like some modern firms, to run up big debts and to rely overmuch upon credit, but on the whole the church was very skilful in its financial operations — it is now many years since Snape pointed out that the monasteries in England were recovering strongly when Henry VIII dissolved them.

What we would like to know most of all is the extent to which the attitudes common amongst churchmen infiltrated the consciousness of laymen, particularly of agricultural workers and their landlords. That great lay landowners had the same accounting practices as the church is now very clear. There is nothing of lay, non-royal origin as early as the Winchester Pipe Roll of 1208, but royal and ecclesiastical example alike were responsible for the gradual adoption of careful accounting and the same stress upon arithmetic amongst lay landlords by the second half of the thirteenth century. Reginald Lennard has demonstrated that the improving lay landlord was a phenomenon well known at the time of Domesday.[7] In spite of old conventions the lay lord was something much more than a giver of rings by the high middle ages.

But what about the poor peasant or, even more so, the thriving kulak whom we have learnt to recognise at all periods between the thirteenth and sixteenth centuries in England? How did the rising peasant, thriving into the yeomanry, and even into the gentry, come to rise and thrive? The very existence of serfdom, free and unfree socage, and freeholding ensured that humble men could take initiatives if they had energy and ability. At all times since the seventh century there had been a tendency for slavery to merge into serfdom, for serfdom to improve, and for freedom to come out of serfdom. Times of reaction, such as the high farming period of the thirteenth century, when good profits in wheat and wool persuaded great landlords to exact work services which they had formerly been willing to let slip for a money payment, were succeeded by times of opportunity, such as the golden age of the European peasantry after the great plagues of the fourteenth century.

But even more than this there is again the influence of the church which worked through the daily routine of the countryman. The Christian religion fitted the rural life very well and the great festivals of the church corresponded exactly with the movements of nature, but even more important was the historical nature of the Christian religion. All depended upon certain events which had happened (or which people thought had happened) in Palestine in the time of Augustus Caesar — the

[7] Reginald Lennard, *Rural England 1086-1135*, Oxford, 1959.

Annunciation, the Nativity, the Passion and Resurrection of Jesus
Christ. Of all the great world religions Christianity is the one most
closely tied to historical events; to be a Christian means belief in these
historical events and their significance; the basic documents of Christianity are historical accounts of events. For this reason a religion which
prided itself upon its otherworldliness, whose eyes were fixed upon
eternity, had to spend great efforts upon historical activity, upon the
events of this world, and was especially favourable to the evolution of
historical method and the study of chronology. Unlike Hindus and
Buddhists, Christians could not ignore the past and were most interested
in the correct ascertainment of the times and seasons at which they
celebrated the past events of their religion. And so we have the avid
medieval concentration upon the calendar and its careful co-ordination
with the rural year.

The greater feasts of the Christian year marked the pattern of rural
life. At the end of summer came autumn, with the Feast of St Michael
the Archangel, and with the harvest completed the medieval ploughman
began the autumn ploughing and sowed wheat and oats. Christmas
marked the end of this season and many manors had a break of up to a
fortnight (or, very commonly, twelve days) until after the Feast of the
Epiphany when Plough Monday celebrated the start of the winter
ploughing, which continued at least until Easter and sometimes until
Whitsuntide. First they planted barley and other crops and then, until
June, ploughed, and perhaps reploughed, the fallow. The start of the
new spring season was usually the Feast of the Annunciation (Lady Day,
25 March), when the grass in normal seasons began to grow and the
animals could go out into pasture. The meadows were then put in
defence and the hay was thus left free from being devoured. The hay
harvest generally preceded the corn harvest and the harvest season itself
was generally the months of August and September, that is, between
1 August (called Lammastide, the Gules of August or the Feast of St
Peter ad Vincula) and Michaelmas (29 September) again. Thus the
Christian calendar fitted rural life and the great feasts of the church had
an echo in pagan fertility beliefs. Christ and John Barleycorn were
buried at about the same time and there is an ancient folk song which
suggests that the medieval peasant was not unaware of the resemblance
between these two figures.

The system of bailiffs, and reeves (or messors) who accounted to the
lord reinforced the peasant's own instinctive belief in the virtues of
thrift, hard work, economy and careful planning which the lord had to
practise in order to make a sound profit. Working a farm through a

bailiff has always been difficult and the medieval bailiff was often illiterate and kept a tally of the sacks of wheat which issued from the barn on the door post of the barn door. The manorial official was also out for his own profit and cheated as often as he could. Chaucer makes this clear about the reeve in his Prologue:

Wel coude he kepe a gerner and a binne;
Ther was noon auditour coude on him winne.
Wel wiste he, by the droghte, and by the reyn,
The yelding of his seed, and of his greyn.
His lordes sheep, his neet, his dayerye,
His swyn, his horse, his stoor, and his pultreye,
Was hoolly in this reves governing,
And by his covenaunt yaf the rekening,
Sin that his lord was twenty year of age;
Ther coude no man bringe him in arrerage.
Ther nas baillif, ne herde, ne other hyne,
That he ne knew his sleighte and his covyne;
They were adrad of him, as of the deeth.

Chaucer was well aware of the medieval method of accounting. The account was between the reeve or bailiff and the lord and debited the reeve with all the rents, services and other forms of income which the lord was due to receive. Against this the account set the *allocationes,* which consisted of the actual expenses which the reeve had incurred in his lord's service, and the actual money which he paid into the lord's treasury. The difference was the *arreragia* (Chaucer's arrerage) which the reeve would, unless excused, have eventually to find out of his own pocket. Reeves were normally serfs and often held office for some years, so that the reeve did not have to answer for his debts until the office changed hands. In payment the reeve received certain privileges, particularly in pasture rights for his horse, and on many manors there was an additional, official tenement which the reeve held. He also as a rule had better food, eating in the lord's hall, at least during the harvest months and sometimes at other times. Opportunities for peculation and speculation were alike present. 'Sold because they were rotten', is the triumphant note about some bushels of barley in one of the Wellingborough account rolls of the Abbey of Crowland towards the end of the thirteenth century. This sort of deceit was probably rather common. Those who wish may sympathise with the poor inhabitants of Llandeilo in West Wales in 1304-5:

From a certain custom on ale, called *tolsester*, received in the vill of Llandeilo, and belonging to my Lord the Prince nothing this year, because the ale made this year in that vill and almost throughout the country was so abominable that it could not be sold.

There were times when the ingenuity even of the medieval Welshman broke down and he had to admit defeat. Direct comment of the peasant upon his condition does not exist except in the form of apocalyptic beliefs and the preachings of heretics and revolutionaries like John Ball. From the actions of the peasant, his careful economy and his wish to rise in the world when opportunity afforded, the historian may deduce that some at least of the virtues of economic man were current in the middle ages, at least from the thirteenth century onwards, among the humbler folk. For the rest, without having recourse to the study of Italian cities and their merchants, which were quite atypical of most of Europe, it is clear that the medieval Latin church was the seed-bed of the early modern idea of capitalism. By the fifteenth century materialism had so extended itself within the church that even the virtues of the saints were a treasury of merit upon which the papacy could draw to pay for the sins of others. The very idea of redemption — the payment which a lord makes for a slave — has in it something fiscal from which the Christian cannot escape. Pelagius objected so strongly to Augustine's notion of God's grace because *gratia* was the undeserved favour which a corrupt lord did for a client. By the fifth century materialism was hard-grained within the Christian tradition, for it was a part of ancient Rome which Christians could not cast out and Benedict and Gregory alike were unwittingly stained by it. The papacy, new western monarchies of the twelfth and thirteenth centuries, and monasticism, were the means by which the capitalist mentality took hard hold upon Europe. Roman materialistic legalism and bureaucracy won out in the end against Christian otherworldliness.

2

On the Ruins
of Feudalism—
Capitalism?

F. J. West

It is a rare occasion that persuades medieval historians, at least outside eastern Europe, to consider Marx's and Engels' views on feudal society. For medieval historians, more perhaps than most professional historians, hold to the custom of the intellectual judgment of their peers. In precise terms this means that they use or build on the work of other medievalists who meet the standards of craftsmanship commonly accepted within the profession. Marx and Engels do not. Who, in learned footnotes, ever refers to them among medieval historians? One result of this assumption that Marx and Engels have nothing of substance to contribute to professional history is that, at conferences, western and eastern European historians scarcely seem to speak the same language. Still, if we remove the discussion from the professional level of medieval history to the history of ideas, what Marx and Engels had to say about feudalism becomes important as a theory of historical change from feudal to capitalist society, and even more important as a reflection, the intellectual superstructure, of nineteenth-century attitudes towards the past which exist as an often unrecognised legacy even among medieval historians.

When Marx and Engels discussed the origins of capitalism, they regularly employed a phrase which is the title of this paper. Capitalism, they say, grew out of the ruins of feudalism. Feudal society they conceived as an aristocracy dominating, and supported by, an unfree, servile peasantry which was quite different from a proletariat because it did not work for wages but as a matter of obligation, and whose labour was in any case unspecialised. The peasantry was not a class that could challenge the feudal lords. This challenge came from the bourgeoisie, from the towns. Marx and Engels considered the guilds of craftsmen as the agencies of challenge to the feudal order, but distinguished them from

the proletariat because the things they produced to satisfy the aristocratic demand for more than subsistence produce were made with their
own tools and were personally produced and identifiable products. This
was not, in their view, the origin of capitalism, although the guilds were
associated with the towns where there grew up a bourgeois class of
entrepreneurs, of lawyers, the *noblesse de la robe*, of rich citizens who
felt the constraints of feudal aristocratic control and who, once the
Reformation had shattered the sacral character of feudalism, challenged
its political control. From the bourgeoisie there developed the capitalist
class and the industrial proletariat. This is in essence the model Marx
and Engels had of feudalism and the way in which capitalism grew out
of its ruins.

One need not stress that it is an economic model of feudalism which
derives social organisation from the mode of production and explains
change in terms of alterations in that mode. But it is worth stressing
that it is precisely because it is an economic model that medieval histori-.
ans do not take it seriously as a description of pre-capitalist society. Of
course some historians do not take the concept of feudalism seriously,
because it is an abstraction which distorts the past by the uniformity it
seems to impose on very diverse conditions throughout Europe and
England, and still more because this abstraction is often used to describe
societies other than European — Japanese, Chinese, Turkish, Russian — in
order to compare them, so that the term loses all precision of meaning.
Yet feudalism is still a useful term for the historian for one particular
reason: there was a period of time in western Europe when men called
themselves feudal men. By this they meant something precise; they
meant the relationships created by a form of real property: the *feudum*
(from which the abstraction feudalism, *feodalité*, was used by a French
nobleman, the Comte de Boulainvilliers in 1727 to describe not simply
legal relationships but the whole society in which the *feudum* or fief
was so important an institution).

The word *feudum* itself is a relatively late invention. It was used by
contemporaries in the twelfth century but not before, and it worked its
way into official and legal terminology from a colloquial status. In
Hainault, a charter of the year 1087 describes a form of property holding,
the benefice, *beneficium*, 'which in vulgar language is called *feudum*'.
The root of the word is generally accepted as that of the German *Vieh*,
cattle, a word which was extended in some of the Frankish areas of
Europe to include any kind of moveable property. In this sense, *feos*,
fees, was used in one of the charters of the abbey of Cluny to describe
the sale of a piece of land where the purchaser could not raise the whole

of the amount in cash so 'we have received from you the agreed price in *feos* valued at' so many pounds, shillings and pence. The *feos* in question were, as other charters make clear, arms, clothing, horses and sometimes food. Detached from this Frankish root, Latinised as *feudum*, the term came to mean land which was given as payment for services. Used in this way in the eleventh century, it had come by the twelfth to replace the older word *beneficium* as the term for a real property right.

Beneficium was a form of landholding taken by the Franks who settled in the ruins of the western Roman empire from the Roman law they found in Gaul. It was a tenement, a piece of land, given by the grantor to a tenant who enjoyed possession and usufruct but not ownership, which was preserved to the grantor. It was called a benefice to distinguish the favourable terms upon which it was held by the tenant, for it carried no labour dues or servile services; the rent was moderate or perhaps non-existent. The reasons for granting a benefice on such favourable tenure varied: to bring waste land into cultivation, to secure the goodwill of an influential person, to recognise a forcible occupation while preserving the final ownership for the future. Such benefices were common enough in the Merovingian kingdom of the Franks in the seventh and eighth centuries.

Feudum ousted *beneficium* as the term for this kind of landholding for two main reasons. In Merovingian Gaul a benefice might be granted for a whole range of services which it became useful to distinguish between. *Feudum* was used to distinguish military service owed for land, the honourable service as a heavy cavalryman, the knight, who became the significant fighting man of the army and the technical answer to the kind of raids upon western Europe made by Vikings, Saracens and Magyars. But it also became necessary to distinguish between land held by a man who was bound to his lord by the personal link of commendation or homage and fealty as distinct from any less solemn relationship. The *feudum* was thus a particular kind of benefice fused with a particular personal relationship. But the personal relationship had in origin no necessary connection with land at all.

Tacitus, in his book on Germany, described the following of a chief, the armed band of retainers, the *comitatus*, the companions whom the chief supported and who followed him even to death. Many great men in the later Roman empire had bands of retainers and dependants which the unsettled conditions of the time made useful or necessary. With the barbarian settlements in Gaul, these groups of armed retainers remained, under the protection of a chief who supported and maintained them and whom they followed in war and whom they served at all times. These people in the sixth and seventh centuries were called by contemporaries *ingenui in obsequio*, free men in dependence, whose Latinised Frankish name was *gasindi*, a term originally meaning companions. *Gasindi* was gradually replaced by another title, *gwassawl*, a Celtic word taken into Latin as *vassallus*, a vassal, perhaps even before the Frankish invasions but certainly before the time of Clovis, the Merovingian king who established the Frankish kingdom in Gaul. *Gwassawl* meant one who served, and it was in this humble sense that it was first Latinised. Until the eighth century it still carried this connotation of a slave but then it began to be extended to those who were dependent upon a lord while retaining their free status, and finally it came to mean armed retainers who were free and honourable men. These changes in meaning illustrate the emergence of a class of vassals who had commended themselves to a lord, and in the Merovingian kingdom of the Franks there existed formulae by which this commendation might take place. The abstract word *commendatio* was seldom if ever used, but the verb *se commendare*, to commend oneself, was frequent. By this act a man placed himself under the authority of a lord with a formal and solemn ceremony. Commendation established a set of obligations binding both parties; upon the lord protection and maintenance, upon the vassal service and respect *(obedientia et reverentia)* so long as these obligations were consistent with his status as a free man. This personal relationship, common in a time of chronic insecurity when lords needed soldiers and men needed protection, was a mutual contract, solemnly undertaken by a vassal's kneeling before his lord, placing his hands in his and swearing to be his faithful man, to shun all that he shunned, to hate all that he hated, until death do us part, or words to that effect. The contract was general in its terms, but it was binding upon both parties. It established the link of lord and man which could be dissolved only by death.

Under the Carolingian kings who succeeded the Merovingians in Gaul in the course of the eighth century, this personal relationship began to combine with a real property relationship. Benefice and vassalage began to fuse. The obligation upon a lord to support and maintain his vassal began to be discharged not only by the gifts of arms, horses and clothing but by a grant of land for the vassal to sustain himself, and a vassal's obligation began to be a condition for obtaining a benefice. The reasons for this development — the expansion of Frankish territorial rule and the deliberate policy of Carolingian kings — need not detain us, but the effect was a slow process of fusion of two separate institutions. It operated from above by a lord's seeking vassals to maintain or extend his power in times of insecurity, and from below with free men seeking protection and maintenance for themselves and their land. By the early ninth century this association of benefice and vassalage was common-place and, more important, a legal connection began to emerge. Louis the Pious declared in 815 that a vassal was bound to use the resources of his benefice to furnish the service which he owed his lord in virtue of the personal relationship commendation had established, and it is equally clear that the grant of a benefice lapsed upon the death of either the lord or the vassal. The ending of the personal relationship involved the ending of the property right. When Charles the Great died in 814, in the eyes of the law the service due from a vassal was then the immediate consideration (to use an English legal term) or cause of the grant of a benefice, and if the service were rendered badly the consideration vanished and the grant of the benefice might be revoked. It was the presence of these two separate institutions which gradually led to *feudum* displacing *beneficium*, as the first became the common, and in some areas the only, form of tenement. As the French lawyers said eventually: *nulle terre sans seigneur*. There was no land without a lord.

Because the characteristic institution of feudal society came from this fusion of a personal relationship with a real property right, histori-ans have been tempted to stress one or the other element as *the* essential one of feudalism, but the fact is that these elements varied in their rela-tive importance. In the Carolingian kingdom it is undoubtedly true that the lord-vassal relationship was more important than the fief as the link which held society together, for while no one but a vassal obtained a benefice, there were many vassals who did not obtain them; it was not invariable or inevitable that a vassal should be supported by a grant of land. And much land was in any case held in other ways than as a bene-fice. Gradually, however, the property element grew in importance, and it began to modify the personal relationship. Most obviously this hap-pened over the question of heritability. If a vassal were to perform his service, to maintain himself by the grant of land, it was essential that the benefice be not diminished or divided, that it should pass on as an entity to another vassal, otherwise the service and the lord's rights suf-fered. In theory, because the personal contract between lord and vassal was terminated by the death of either, the benefice was held for the term of a single life; and in strict law this principle remained. Yet as a matter of custom from an early date following the fusion of personal and property elements, a vassal who had gained a benefice because of his own particular qualities might succeed in obtaining a regrant of his fief from the heir of his original lord, and a vassal might also try to secure that his fief passed to his own heir. Either of these eventualities diminished the authority of a lord — the Carolingian kings in fact tried to stop both practices without much success — and in so doing the relationship of lord and vassal was altered by the interest which the property element created. The heritability of benefices had become common enough by the end of the ninth century. In the year 868 the Archbishop of Rheims told Charles the Bald that 'when a bishop granted a benefice to a man from the property of the church in return for military service, he is bound to give it to the sons if they are fitted to succeed their father'. The effect of this conjunction of property and personal relationships was thus slowly to give more weight to the *feudum* than to the lord-man link. By the recognition of the hereditary character of a benefice, the rights of the vassal were strengthened against the lord and the personal bond therefore changed its character.

It was not only the change resulting from the fusion. The benefice or *feudum* produced two other consequences for the personal element. The first was that the desire for more property, for more benefices or fiefs, led men into becoming vassals of a number of lords. Whereas the original bond between lord and man was unique, its association with land led to the lord-vassal ties being duplicated or multiplied, and this multiplication of personal engagements weakened any single one of them by the conflicting duties and obligations it set up. What if the interests of two of a man's lords clashed? To whom did he owe his allegiance? Conversely which of a man's lords would take responsibility for him? The church of St Martin of Tours experienced the effects of this difficulty in the year 895 when one of the vassals of the Count of Le Mans vexed them. But upon their complaint the count replied that they should appeal to another lord of the vassal concerned of whom he also held a benefice: 'because he was much more the vassal [of this other lord] . . . since he held of the latter a much larger benefice'. Obviously the personal relationship had weakened towards the end of the ninth century; multiple allegiances were becoming common. But the Count of Le Mans' reply to the clergy of St Martin of Tours also introduces the second change set in motion by the association of personal and property relationships: the connection between the size of a benefice and the obligations due. In other words, the amount of land was beginning to determine the service; the personal bond was ceasing to do so. By the end of the ninth century the size of the benefice was coming to be the condition of service.

The final result of this fusion of *feudum* and vassalage was to reverse their relative importance. From the dominance of the personal relationship the property element had, by the eleventh century, come to be the aspect contemporaries stressed. A fief was then the cause of entering into a contract of vassalage, not its result. In 1039, a baron who became a vassal of a bishop said, in swearing fealty, that his faith would hold 'as long as I shall be your vassal and shall hold your land'. In law, the reciprocal duties of lord and man were still created by the personal bond, by the act of homage and the oath of fealty into which a property consideration did not enter, but in practice it was the *feudum* that mattered. By the tenth century even the solemn ritual of homage and fealty, of becoming the man of a lord and swearing an oath of faith, took cognisance of the fact of property. The English lawyer Bracton reveals this in the formula he supplies for the solemn ceremony: 'I become your man in respect of the tenement which I hold of you'. By this date, too, the service that one who became a vassal ought to render had come to be regarded not as a personal obligation incurred in virtue of commendation, but as an incident of the *feudum* itself; the land was burdened with service, not the man. In the hands of Roman lawyers these changes reached the point at which the lord-vassal contract without a *feudum*, a piece of real property joined to it, lacked a cause or, in English legal phraseology, a consideration and was therefore null and void.

Such were the origins and development of the *feudum*, the property form which lent its name to the characterisation of a society. And until the eighteenth century, lawyers and scholars who talked of feudal laws meant the rules which governed the relationships created by the fief. Thus the word feudal had a precise and technical meaning, however much the lawyers and antiquarians squabbled over the Germanic or Roman origin of the fief and however much English common lawyers' insularity sought to play down the English debt to this continental fief. The *feudum* was placed in the forefront at the centre of society; this is why that society could, by extension of meaning, be called feudal: because it contained the fief. Yet even this precise definition involved some distortion. From what I have said about the origins and development of the *feudum* it is clear that to stress, as the sixteenth- and seventeenth-century lawyers did, the real property element distorted the place of the lord-man element of the earlier stages in the fief's history. The legal definition was too narrow to cover the full reality of the *feudum* and it obscured the dual nature of its development by defining it in terms of what it was in its later stages. To use the word feudal, therefore, to mean the society in which the fief was so important an element, involves some distortion because it imposes a static quality on something which in fact markedly changed. But it is the closest to precision that a term like feudalism can come. It is the sense in which historians who find the term useful must therefore have considerable reservations about Marx's and Engels' model of feudalism from the ruins of which capitalism sprang.

For, in outlining in some detail how western medieval historians commonly saw feudal society, it has not once been necessary to discuss the manorial system, the economic organisation of society. Yet it is the manorial system, the lords and the unfree peasantry that Marx and Engels mean by feudalism, and in their view the 'feudalisation' of society means the subjection of free peasants to this military aristocracy. This kind of feudal society could not produce capitalism, for the two classes in it are passive, fixed by custom; roles and methods are all 'given'; the environment is 'constant' and 'custom' is an obstacle to change. Hence capitalism could develop only on the ruin of such a society, a ruin worked by a new class, the bourgeoisie of the towns whose interest was not in passivity but in change, not in custom but in contract, which Marx and Engels assumed to be the polarity of 'custom'. Nevertheless, the manorial system, meaning by that an estate divided between the lord's land and tenant land, long antedates feudal society and long survived it. The Roman Ausonius describes, in a poem, an estate organised in the same way that the 'classic' feudal manor was. But the distinctive feature of the feudal manor lay not in its economic organisation, but in external circumstances: the absence of a state which provided an army and a system of judicial courts, so that the feudal lord was both warrior and judge of his own men in his own court. Those men were, many of them (but far from all), 'unfree'. But that term is a legal definition, not an economic one; it tells one nothing about the prosperity or the size of the landholding of the unfree person. Nor does it tell one about the absence of wage labour or about money rents instead of labour services. For the feudal manor consisting of lord with his demesne land cultivated by unfree peasants as a matter of obligation, and the tenures on which these tenants supported themselves, may not even have been typical of the manorial economy which Marx and Engels identify with feudalism. Most recent research, including Kosminsky's, shows very great variety, including the fact that many manors could not possibly have been worked by an unfree labour force, that money rents must have paid for wage labour, even when, for example with the Norman conquest of England, society was strictly feudal as a result of that arbitrary settlement.

Even, therefore, if one could accept the identification of feudalism with the manorial system, it would be hard for most medieval economic historians to use a model which took no account of the diversity which existed at any given time and of the changes which occurred over a period of time. The feudal lords of the eleventh century may very well have lived largely on the produce of their estates, taking a sufficiency, not a profit, but by the thirteenth century when, in contemporary satire, a warrior might pore over his accounts to amass capital rather than go off to fight, the improving lord might well try to reimpose labour services because he had become more interested in his land than in his feudal duties as a knight. One reason for this change was, of course, that the necessity to raise a heavy cavalry force to cope with heathen invasions of western Europe vanished when the attacks not only ceased but Europe went over to the offensive in the crusades against those who had formerly attacked it. The feudal lords could become landed gentlemen during the thirteenth century. And as landed gentlemen they could change the organisation of their estates under pressures such as inflation, overpopulation, the demand for wool and the like. On this view, change came not so much from the towns and the bourgeoisie as a rising class, but from the feudal lords themselves, who after all controlled the principal source of wealth: land. Indeed, towns and markets, often a deliberate creation of a feudal lord rather than a hostile and alien growth in feudal society, were an important source of his income.

The changes which altered feudal society, so far as they are not external ones such as the disappearance of the external threats to Europe, came rather from the feudal lords than from a class challenge to them, certainly in England. For the royal administration, as it was elaborated from the twelfth century onwards, by making feudal lords out of capable royal officials, constantly introduced men accustomed to innovation into estate management. And so, of course, did the promotion into bishoprics and abbeys of royal clerks who thus became feudal lords. Becket who, as Archbishop of Canterbury was the greatest of feudal lords, was the son of a London merchant. Four of the justiciars, the king's viceroys, came from very modest beginnings to become great barons within the twelfth century. This recruitment into the ranks of feudal lords came through achieving a position as a useful servant in the royal court, which thus becomes one of the most important agencies of change within feudal society, rather than class conflict.

But having argued that the Marx and Engels model of the origins of capitalism does not fit what medieval historians know of feudal society and the manorial economy, that it wrongly identifies the agencies of change within either or both, one might ask: why should it fit? As a model it was first developed in the mid-nineteenth century before the major, recognisably professional historical work had been done on feudal society. That revolution in historiography which replaced romantic views of a free Germanic past or of the Catholic centuries — the romantic medievalism common enough in Marx's student days — did not happen until the last quarter of the nineteenth century. Since Marx and Engels show no sign of familiarity with seventeenth- and early eighteenth-century works by what are often called the antiquarians — Pappenheim or Mabillon, Madox or Spelman or Dugdale — the material for any real knowledge of feudal society was lacking. None of the writers cited in *Capital*, for example, would be regarded by medieval historians as an intellectual peer. No model is better than the material out of which it is constructed, and Marx and Engels simply did not have good medieval materials. What they had was the pattern that seemed to be supplied by the French Revolution. The revolutionaries who in August 1789 declared that they had utterly abolished the feudal regime obviously established the bourgeois revolution on the ruins of the feudalism they said they had overthrown. Such a pattern of revolution, in the context of the mid-nineteenth-century search for the laws governing society as well as those of physical creation, seems to me to explain the Marx and Engels model, not a study of the feudal past. Such laws, as an explanatory model, provided Marx and Engels with a view of historical causation, which is chiefly interesting to an historian of the ideas of nineteenth-century Europe rather than to the historian of the feudal past. Or, I suspect, the historian of the origins of capitalism, a term which distorts the past quite as much as does feudalism itself, when used by analogy with the natural sciences to explain a social evolution which is believed, *a priori*, to exist.

3

Early Modern Capitalism—
the Augustan Perception

J. G. A. Pocock

In this paper I shall focus upon an episode in the history of ideas strictly so defined. That is, I shall be concerned with the emergence of the idea of capitalism, or at least with the Augustan perception of something which may be worth calling capitalism, though the Augustans themselves employed other names for it; and I shall attempt to show what elements in Augustan perceived experience and what elements in Augustan modes of perceiving experience accounted for the emergence of this perception. I shall work on the assumption — which I shall also attempt to justify — that the reigns of William III and Anne, in England and Great Britain, present us with the first occasion on which secular social criticism, operating on the whole in non-religious terms, became engrossed with the rise of an expansive modern economy, possessing non-traditional institutions visibly its own, and with the impact of differing and changing forms of property upon political society and the civic personality. All this perception really happened — to use the historian's basic formula — and it is clearly of importance to see how.

But a seminar with such a title as this is bound to become in some measure a debate about Marxist and non-Marxist methodologies, and it may be desirable at this stage to outline a number of ways in which mine diverges from certain Marxist norms as I understand them. Conventional Marxism is concerned with a supposed transition from 'feudal' to 'bourgeois' and from 'manor' to 'market' and it presents contemporary perceptions of this transition, as based upon perception of the displacement of the image of the individual performing traditional services in a manor by an image of him operating as a buyer and seller in a market. I am going to argue that perception of social change in the period I shall discuss was not based upon the perceived rise of the individual as market operator or merchant in the simple entrepreneurial sense (and indeed that the merchant was a neutral and almost irrelevant figure, acceptable to all parties), but upon perception of changes in the role of the individual as citizen, performing his public functions both political and military. The crucial institutions in and through which change was seen to be proceeding were not the economy or productive relationships or even agrarian landholding society, but parliament and army. I shall argue that, as the individual — *qua* propertied individual — was not seen primarily as changing his productive so much as his public behaviour, perception of this change did not come in the form of a new theory of liberal and acquisitive individualism, of which Locke was supposedly the prophet, to nearly the extent that has been suggested. Indeed, what is sometimes called 'bourgeois ideology', far from making its appearance as a simple and immediate perception of changed productive relationships, fought its way into being, not merely in the teeth of ideological opposition, but in the face of bitter moral and philosophical perplexities, themselves occasioned by the continuing strength of ideas that were in no useful sense either traditional or feudal in character. In short, I shall suggest that perceptions of capitalism in this period emerged in ways significantly different from those normally supposed by liberal Marxist orthodoxy and that the relation of perception to social change is less simple and mirror-like than the verb 'reflects' has commonly suggested.

The material I shall present is based upon a chapter in my book, *The Machiavellian Moment*,[1] the relevant chapter title being 'Neo-Machiavellian political economy; the Augustan debate over land, trade and credit'. I do not want to spend too much space here explaining why it was that Machiavellian ideas, at a late stage in their history, became tools for isolating the problems created by the incursion of money into political culture, but this is in fact the reason why these problems were discussed in a context of politics rather than production. Whether or not one thinks he deserved to be, Machiavelli was for the late seventeenth and eighteenth centuries a principal transmitter of the ideals and technical theory of what can be termed either civic humanism or classical republicanism.[2] This revived the ancient assertion that man was by nature a citizen, fulfilling his virtue — an extremely pregnant term — in participation in a self-governing republic, hierarchical in the sense that its members possessed differing qualifications and capacities, egalitarian

[1] *The Machiavellian Moment: the Florentine contribution to the Atlantic republican tradition. A study in the politics of time*, Princeton University Press, 1975, ch.13.

[2] See the present writer's *Politics, Language and Time*, London, 1971, and contribution to M. Fleisher (ed.), *Machiavelli and the Nature of Political Thought*, New York, 1972.

in the sense that each member must rule and be ruled, respecting the special qualities of others as they respected his. If this ideal was to be realised, each citizen must possess sufficient moral and material autonomy to ensure that his actions were his own and the republic's, and were not at the unchallenged command of any other man or group of men. If he was economically dependent, he was a servant and no citizen; if he was a citizen and social relations changed so that he became politically dependent on another, then the relations between citizens composing the republic had become corrupt. Moral and material autonomy was therefore necessary if the individual was to be a citizen and, since it was the fulfilment of human nature to be one, the highly politicised virtue of the citizen — his capacity for equality and civic action — was necessary to his moral and psychological health. To lose autonomy, to lose freedom, to lose equality was to lose an essential component of the personality, and the corruption of the republic was the corruption of the personality of the citizen. To become dependent on another was to part with an element of one's self; to this extent the concept of corruption anticipates that of alienation.

The material basis for civic personality had for Aristotle been represented by the household or *oikos*, from which our word economics is, of course, derived. In ruling his women, children and servants, the citizen obtained his first lesson in ruling, which qualified him to rule and be ruled among his equals; and to live in and rule his own household ensured that he should not live and be ruled in that of another. But Machiavelli, for reasons it would take too long to go into, had to a considerable degree shifted the emphasis from the notion of the household to that of arms. If the individual owned his arms, he could bear them in the republic's cause and be a citizen; if he owned or bore them only in subjection to another individual — either as a feudal retainer or as a hired mercenary — he could not be a citizen; and if too many men occupied this status there could not be a republic. The decline of the arms-bearer to client status was to Machiavelli the paradigmatic case of the corruption and decline of a republic — the transition from the Rome of Camillus and Cincinnatus to the Rome of Pompey and Caesar; and the presence or absence of a citizens' militia was the acid test of freedom and the main cause of the rise and decline of republics and human virtue.

The moral ambiguities Machiavelli detected and explored in this conception of virtue lie apart from the theme we are now following, which is that the concept of arms, used in this way, became crucial in developing a sociology of liberty for pre-industrial political theorists. It was clear, of course, that there were economic pre-requisites to the indivi-

dual's possession of his own arms. One of Machiavelli's strongest arguments for the superiority of the citizen militia over hired mercenaries
is that the citizen, having a home of his own, will fight to win in order
to get back to it, whereas the mercenary, having no home but the camp,
will not fight to win since he does not care if the war never ends.
Property in this projection still serves a primarily moral purpose; it is a
guarantee of virtue and there is no suggestion that you become more
virtuous by increasing your property. Machiavelli seems indeed to have
retained a classical suspicion of wealth and luxury, as tending to dis-
tract men from virtue by increasing the number of secondary goods
before their eyes, and he does not echo the statement, rather common
in the *quattrocento*, that Florentines are better citizens because they
are merchants. Virtue in the civic sense was a static and stabilising
element, and Machiavelli did not alter its economic basis in those
respects in which he sought to make it warlike, expansive and dynamic.
It remained a moral quality, exposed to corruption.

The conceptual pattern was deepened, without being fundamentally
changed, in the next century when ideas about the relation of arms to
virtue were found to be highly relevant to the experience of England in
and after the civil wars. There the greatest of neo-Machiavellians is, of
course, James Harrington, who saw that the apparent collapse of parliamentary monarchy could be explained by positing a transition from
a feudal order of barons and vassals to an order of independent freeholders. The feudal order, in which most men fought for a few lords,
could only be oligarchical and, furthermore, unstable — a wrestling
ground, as Harrington put it, between king and nobility — but the society
in which there were many freeholders, independent and equal in the
possession of their own lands and their own arms, was incapable of
being governed in any other way than as a republic. Harrington's famous
dictum that power followed property can therefore be restated as
meaning that land is the basis of arms and arms of civic capacity and
virtue.

It is noteworthy that Harrington described the feudal order as
modern, in the sense of post-classical and degenerate, and saw the freeholders' republic as a return to classical purity. The prime political
model in his mind was therefore civic and participatory, not that of a
liberal democracy in the sense in which twentieth-century socialists use
that term; and the function of property was to ensure personal autonomy, issuing in the exercise of arms and of citizenship. It might perhaps be argued that there is something manorial, if not feudal in the
proper sense of the word, about Harrington's image of the freeholder,

autonomous and independent on his estates and issuing forth in arms to take part in the activities of the republic and display what is once called 'the genius of a gentleman'. But a concern for the classical Marxist transition from feudal to bourgeois, and from manor to market, has led some scholars to probe for bourgeois and market elements in the social relations envisaged as existing between Harrington's post-feudal free-holders; and Professor Macpherson has claimed to have discovered a level of analysis on which Harrington's system does not work well unless we suppose that the freeholders are maintaining an essentially capitalist attitude toward their land.[3] I continue, on the whole, to dissent from this interpretation. Harrington knew well enough that men were acquisitive, bought land, and sometimes sold it to keep up their family position; but to say that they bought it in order to sell it again, or that it was a commodity and a source of profit, is a step which I cannot see that he took. There is a passage in which he concedes that in theory, goods and money could serve as well as land as the basis for civic autonomy; but he adds immediately that the objection to mobile property serving in this capacity is, precisely, its mobility. 'Lightly come, lightly go' is the phrase he uses; what you have acquired by traffic and exchange you can easily lose again, and when property is being treated as the basis of your freedom, your personal autonomy and your capacity for virtue, you do not lightly treat it as a commodity. Harrington knew that there existed a republic in which most men's substance consisted in moveable property rather than in land; this republic, he tells us, is Holland, and if the main thrust of his argument had been to reduce the political relations between men to a species of market relationships, one would have expected him to analyse the relations of power to property among the Dutch. But he nowhere does this and, like most men of his age, he simply does not know how to. Land, or real property, remains the paradigmatic instance of the property which makes us capable of civic action, and other modes of property — in goods, money or office — are admitted insofar as they can be assimilated to it; usury and profit are acceptable in Harrington's system so long as the wealth derived from land is sufficient to outweigh the wealth derived from trade. There is, when all is said and done, an immediate and evident contradiction between the idea of property as the foundation of personality and the idea of property as a marketable commodity; one does not readily take to playing the markets with one's own personality, and the idea that the foundation of one's personality is one's capacity to play the markets, though it has been formulated,

[3] C. B. Macpherson, *The Political Theory of Possessive Individualism*, Oxford, 1962.

was an extremely difficult one to work out. A large part of my argument in this paper is that the history of how it was worked out has yet to be adequately written.

I therefore contend that Harrington's doctrine of property and power remains essentially within the confines of a definition of real property as an inheritable freehold in land. In those passages where he is talking most unequivocally about the acquisitiveness of man, he seems to me to be saying that one acquires wealth for the sake of one's family, which the patriarchal and patrimonial mind of the age saw as a structure perpetuated by generation and inheritance. One acquired — one even bought — less to sell again than to bequeath; and it was more blessed to inherit than to acquire, since it involved one in fewer obligations and dependences. Inheritable property was not only real but natural, and kept the economic sphere subordinate to the biological and physical order, as Burke was still pointing out over a century later. Harrington's economics, in short, appear to me to have been *oikonomika* in the strict Greek sense; an art of creating and perpetuating the household, to which *chrematistika,* the art of acquisition, was contingent rather than essential; and this would not cease to be so if Harrington's chrematistic were shown to include some idea of a market, which it is perfectly possible it does. And if Greek household economics were what Marx meant when he said 'feudal', then I wish we had all known this sooner.

Real rather than mobile property anchored the personality in a durable structure of virtue; as Bolingbroke put it in the next century, the landed men owned the ship and the monied men were merely passengers in it.[4] However, as I shall try to show, when Bolingbroke said 'monied men', he was not thinking primarily of merchants, and the trading entrepreneur was admissible to the realm of virtue insofar as his property could be shown to approach the reality, solidity and naturalness of land. The point which I think has been most neglected, and requires most stressing, is that the merchant is not the crucial figure in shaping early perceptions of what is now called bourgeois society; he had at least two predecessors, and this of course bears upon the inexactitude which renders terms like 'bourgeois' and 'middle class' unsatisfactory to the historian. What was going on in mid-seventeenth-century England was the measurement of social types to see if they conformed to the paradigm of civic autonomy and personality; the notion of virtue was becoming increasingly paramount, and that of independence in arms was gaining rather than losing in conceptual importance. These

[4] Isaac F. Kramnick, *Bolingbroke and His Circle: the politics of nostalgia in the age of Walpole*, Cambridge, Mass., 1968.

were the criteria used to identify and evaluate — negatively — the emerging social types who did not conform and so threatened society with corruption. These in turn were indeed defined and denounced by their property; but since independence was the criterion, the social analysts of the age were interested in modes of property which seemed to entail undue dependence upon others and upon government, and this was not a reproach obviously to be brought against the merchant.

It would not have been surprising if the ideas of Harrington had vanished for ever at the Restoration of 1660. He had premised that the monarchy and the House of Lords had perished with the disappearance of feudal tenure; but both institutions were restored when feudal tenure was not. However, before this happened, Harrington's concepts were being used to analyse a phenomenon of a different kind: what seemed an attempt by grandees of the dying New Model Army to entrench themselves in the constitution as life peers in an upper house.[5] What was attacked here was the notion that men dependent on government for office and salary should have guaranteed voices in voting the money from which such salaries were to be paid; and office thus became a principal mode of property denounced, in the language of virtue and corruption, for entailing dependence in the proprietor and an exercise of power on his part which was corrupt less because it was interested — this I think is important — than because it was dependent.

This critique could be extended, and was, to the civilian placeman as well as to the military officer; and about the time of Harrington's death in 1677, there was going on a vigorous revival and revision of his ideas which we now refer to as neo-Harringtonianism.[6] An important element in the revision referred to is that the freeholders' commonwealth is now located in the past, in a state of society usually termed 'Gothic', when free men owned their own lands, bore their own arms and did their own governing; this image has clearly been built up by divesting the medieval order of its strictly feudal component — the subordination of vassal to lord which had been of such significance to Harrington in his endeavour to locate the freeholders' commonwealth in classical antiquity and in an imminent revolutionary future. 'Gothic liberty', as the neo-Harringtonians came to call it, was seen as surviving into the present, but as desperately threatened by corruption in the sense of the growth of a new technique of government which took the form of patronage, of using civil and military office, and the funds attendant on it, to weaken

[5]J. G. A. Pocock, 'James Harrington and the Good Old Cause: a study of the context of his political thought', *Journal of British History*, 1971.

[6]*Politics, Language and Time*, ch.4.

the parliaments of freeholders by establishing in them increasing numbers of officers and pensioners dependent on the state for their substance. A vital role in this corruptive procedure was played by the growth of standing armies — not the freely contracting condottieri of medieval and Renaissance times, but salaried servants of the state supported and paid by bureaucracies both civil and military. The true standing army — something which the New Model had never quite become — was dreaded less as an instrument of dictatorship than as one of corruption; and this dread became obsessive even in advance of the standing army's admittedly rapid growth, in a very interesting illustration of the way in which conceptual structures can grow faster than the phenomena which immediately occasion them. Social consciousness is something far more complex than a mirror.

This line of argument was vigorously advanced between 1675 and about 1680, but lapsed during the monarchist ascendancy of the 1680s; nor did it play any significant part in the justification, or the denunciation, of the events of 1688-9. Whatever James II was doing, it was something far cruder than the corruption of society through the creation of indirect dependencies; and in any case, the analysis of corruption was something distinct from the controversy as to whether obedience was an absolute or a conditional obligation. If one thinks of Locke's *Two Treatises of Government* as belonging to this controversy, it will help one to understand that Augustan social criticism was framed along lines — the analysis of corruption — to which Locke did not immediately belong, and along which he was often not significantly visible. I am about to pursue a development in the history of social thought which seems to be of great importance and dominant over the intellectual scene of the eighteenth century; and to this debate Locke had indeed an indirect relevance and his language helps to elucidate it; but it was conducted by men who used assumptions which Locke did not share and who did not seem to be alluding to his thought one way or the other. I am stressing this because there is a convention of writing as if Locke dominated the thought of the eighteenth century, and imposed upon it a pattern of liberal individualism which made the state no more than the protector of entrepreneurial activities which it regarded with benign indifference; and both these suppositions I consider very wide of the mark.

What actually happened was this. The political revolution of 1688-9 — a bipartisan and somewhat backward-looking affair — had to be paid for with intensive English involvement in the Franco-Dutch wars of the continent, and was followed within a few years by a drastic series of innovations now becoming known as the Financial Revolution,[7] beginning about 1694-6, whose outcome was the erection of a structure of public credit that rendered England capable of waging war as a great power in Europe, for the first time in her modern history. The crucial steps in the Financial Revolution were the foundation of the Bank of England and the institution of the National Debt. Individuals great and small – Locke, by the way, was one of the first of them – were now encouraged to lend money to the government and live off the returns on their capital, thus investing in the future stability of the Revolution. With these loans as its security, the government was enabled to borrow on a yet larger scale and with the funds thus raised to carry out a massive expansion and perpetuation of the professional army and navy, together with the civilian bureaucracies that sustained them and their conquests. It reached the point of embarking upon enterprises and contracting loans that could not be paid off on the security of existing funds, so that repayment had to be secured upon revenues to be raised in the future; but war could not be paid for out of public credit alone, and necessitated a steady rise in taxes, levied for the most part upon land. Finally, under these conditions it was found that the paper guarantees entitling the holder to a share in what the government paid out on its borrowings themselves became a commodity, bought and sold at prices that rose and fell as public confidence in the government's operations waxed and waned – a fluctuation affected by and affecting the volume of trading in the public stocks.

Now it is the reaction to this new and dramatically created edifice of public credit that constitutes what I have called the Augustan perception of capitalism, and it constitutes, certainly, the staple of Augustan social criticism and debate. I have been engaged so far in this paper in establishing the structure of ideas, laid down before 1694, through which Englishmen perceived the Financial Revolution when it came upon them; and my aim has been to show that it ensured that they would interpret so great a change in terms of its impact upon property considered as the foundation of personal autonomy, civic participation and virtue. If the function of property was to render the individual independent and virtuous, real property served that purpose better than mobile, and inherited property better than purchased; the trader in a stock of movable goods or the metal tokens of wealth was, as we have seen, mildly distrusted on the grounds that the foundations of his civic personality were constantly shifting and tended to involve him in too

[7]P. G. M. Dickson, *The Financial Revolution in England: a study in the development of public credit, 1688-1756*, London, 1967.

fluid a nexus of relationships with others. But his wealth was at least his own. That of the salaried officeholder or pensioner was another matter; its essence was dependence upon a paymaster, who might be the state, and for this reason office had become the archetype of those modes of property which were inherently corruptive, and market wealth had not. But the Financial Revolution trebled the types of such property at a single blow, and in the same moment made them supreme in the state. The rentier sustained the government in the act of living off it, and caused the state to be sustained by a vast class of its own dependents. With the capital he contributed, the state could multiply the number of its officers, both military and civil, and could place them in parliament to corrupt the independence of the representatives of property. The stocks which were his title to a return upon the loans he had made became themselves a commodity, and their value was manipulated by a new class of beings called stockjobbers, the most corrupt and parasitic of all, since they were dependent upon the dependence of others and sought seats in parliament to perpetuate the system that brought them there. The Financial Revolution therefore impressed Augustan social critics as the greatest escalation in the means of corruption the world had ever seen — greater, they suspected, than the comparable takeover by corrupt financiers and soldiers that had brought the Roman republic to an end — and they saw it quite definitely as a revolution in the nature of property and in the relations of property to government. But in the order of their perceptions of the modes of property concerned, the officer preceded the rentier, and the rentier the merchant.

In the ensuing debate, which began about 1698 — and which was conducted in significant measure by persons eminent in the production of imaginative literature (so that they are studied today largely in departments of English) — a leading theme is the contrast between the militia of free proprietors, depicted in terms at once Machiavellian and neo-Harringtonian, at once civic and Gothic, and the newly emergent professional army dependent upon the bureaucratic and fiscal efficiency of the state financed for war. John Trenchard and Andrew Fletcher argued that civic freedom was possible only where the proprietors bore their own arms, and drew outlines of a society in which the militia should be the means of educating the freeholding youth in liberty and citizenship.[8] But such an institution they held all the more necessary because the militia had been sustained by the economic workings of

[8]John Trenchard (with Walter Moyle), *An Argument showing that a Standing Army is inconsistent with a Free Government and absolutely destructive of the Constitution of the English Monarchy*, 1697; Andrew Fletcher, *A Discourse of*

society only in the Gothic past. From about the year 1500, they said, commerce and knowledge had been rapidly increasing, with the consequence that, as men became increasingly able to pursue a diversity of moral and intellectual goods, they became increasingly tempted to depute to paid servants the duty of defending their own freedom; but since arms were inseparable from liberty, they gave away their freedom in the act of developing their culture, and the classic pattern of corruption could be seen as repeating itself on a world-historical scale. To this Daniel Defoe and others retorted in terms which were more Harringtonian than those of the neo-Harringtonians themselves. A Gothic society, all land and no trade, had, they said, been one in which most men were subject — between vassal and serf they did not distinguish — to a few lords; the growth of trade — they were more emphatic about this than Harrington himself — had been a necessary part of the process in which the commons had emancipated themselves from the control of the barons; and since there were now representative assemblies commanding the power of the purse, the army paid by the state was not to be dreaded. 'No parliament *his* army could disband', wrote Defoe of William the Conqueror. 'He raised no money, for he paid in land.'[9]

The retort was effective, but in several ways fell short of offering a full alternative to the neo-Harringtonian thesis. It did not provide a clear and acceptable substitute for the classical identification of arms and property with virtue, and so did not deliver Trenchard and Fletcher from the historical contradiction they had themselves posited. If human virtue was civic virtue, and if arms and freehold were necessary to civic virtue, then it remained hard to answer the pessimistic claim that the growth of culture — of commerce, of the arts and of enlightenment — was incompatible with the maintenance of civil freedom and the moral wholeness of the personality. The Rousseauan contradiction had already been outlined, and this had been done — as early as 1698, be it remembered — on lines which clearly supposed a process of historical change based on specialisation and division of labour. The growth of culture, of which commerce was the dynamic, offered men a choice of alternatives denied the Gothic warrior, and tempted them to pay others to exercise vital functions of the civic personality for them. Another step had been taken on the road which developed the concept of corruption into that of alienation; but the governing paradigm was that of the man

---

Government with Relation to Militias, 1698. See Lois G. Schwoerer, 'The Literature of the Standing Army Controversy', *Huntington Library Quarterly*, 1964-5.

[9] *The True-Born Englishman: a Satyr*, 1701.

74

in arms as an essential aspect of the man in citizenship — it was his civic personality, thus defined, that civilised man was tempted to alienate. Trenchard and Fletcher were historical pessimists to the extent that they did not see how he could be prevented from doing this; but their patterns of thought could be replaced only if someone could come forward with a new paradigm of social and historical personality, to replace the paradigm of virtue by showing how the individual might accept increasing specialisation without abandoning his participation in politics, or might abandon a directly participant politics without suffering a decisive loss of personality. Professor Macpherson has been taken to argue that in the year 1700 much of this had already been done; he and I might well agree upon the normative proposition that it has never been done very satisfactorily, but what I want to argue now is that in the eighteenth century it was done, if at all, with very great difficulty, by men who knew that what they were doing was both difficult and unsatisfactory and involved making great sacrifices and accepting many real if necessary evils.

So much may be said concerning the Augustan debate as organised around the problem of the warrior, a debate that continued to be of deep concern at least as late as the Second Amendment to the Constitution of the United States.[10] But I have suggested that the figure of the warrior as officeholder preceded that of the rentier in contemporary social perception, and that of the rentier the merchant; and this is borne out by the circumstance that the Augustan debate, which raged for two generations concerning the corruptive impact of 'the monied interest' or 'commerce' upon civil society, regularly treated the figure of the creditor, the stockholder or stockjobber, as crucial in a way that the figure of the merchant was not. The merchant's property might be too fluid and mobile to serve as a reliable foundation for virtue; his trade, as increasing the opportunities for luxury and choice, specialisation and alienation, might be central in the history of corruption being delineated by men such as Andrew Fletcher. But as long as his wealth appeared to be in some sense real and substantial, the foundations of his civic personality appeared real also; and when doubts arose concerning the reality of monetary wealth and the virtue of the merchant, they arose from consideration of the workings of the credit mechanism. Locke — this is one point at which it is highly relevant to quote him — had considered the change which must have come over the primitive economy when wealth in money was added to wealth in land, and he

[10] 'A well-regulated militia being necessary to the security of a free state, the right of the people to keep and bear arms shall not be abridged'.

had named 'fancy and agreement' as the two psychological forces which had operated to give certain metals a token value for use as symbols in exchange.[11] These two words are of great importance to the understanding of the Augustan debate. Fancy, which may be renamed imagination or passion, and agreement, which may be renamed convention or confidence, gave value to money; and once land was considered as a source of rents rather than services, money gave value to land. But the analysis did not end there. Once a credit mechanism was introduced into the workings of society, the value of money became largely a question of the rate at which it could be borrowed; and this, given the workings of the bank, the funds and the national debt, became largely a question of the market value of stocks, which went up and down with the fluctuations of public confidence but was exposed to manipulation by speculators who bought, sold and spread rumours in the city with a view to creating the changes in public confidence they thought profitable to themselves.

One therefore finds that all Augustan analysts of political economy accept the interdependence of land, trade and credit; and, furthermore, that all agree that land is an important foundation of virtue, stock-jobbing a pernicious means to corruption, and money and trade vital components of national wealth and power. The apologists for land make much of the importance of trade, and claim that stockjobbing is ruinous to the value of both; the apologists for war and credit stress that trade is necessary to the value of land, and deny that stockjobbing alters this relationship; and there are, on the face of it, no apologists for stock-jobbing at all. On one level of interpretation, this means that the argument is less than ingenuous: trade, clearly, is like motherhood — nobody is against it and both factions want to claim it as their own — and the credit mechanism, while defensible as a necessary adjunct of commerce and even liberty, is on the whole the skeleton at the feast, which has to be robed in the decent habiliments of trade if its presence is to be admitted at all. But a corollary to this dialectical dishonesty is that both factions share, not only the same reading of the economic facts, but the same underlying value system, in which the only material foundation for civic virtue and moral personality is taken to be independence and real property. Any move away from the landed or Gothic order was a move in the direction of corruption even when it was historically inevitable, another reason, incidentally, why Machiavellian values, so much concerned with the self-destructive nature of virtue, continued to be para-

[11] John Locke, *Two Treatises of Government*, ed. Peter Laslett, Cambridge, 1960, p.342.

digmatic in stating the Augustan dilemma. And the most striking discovery one makes, in pursuing the thought of this period, is that the admission that credit and commerce tend to the corruption of society is most intelligently and realistically made by Whigs who are concerned to defend credit and commerce, rather than by Tories who are concerned merely to attack them; and even the Tories are at their best when they admit that credit and commerce have come to stay. The retention by both factions of a static value system, according to which the dominant facts of the age were at best a necessary evil, enabled them to analyse that evil more clearly; and we shall see that when an admission of the necessary egoism and amorality of commercial man arose, it arose from men whose ideology drove them to inhabit, and without any illusions, a widening gap between facts and values.

But this reformulation of the social situation was not easy to arrive at, and there were serious epistemological obstacles in its path. Locke's phrase about 'fancy and agreement' appears to offer the key to much that went on. He had named these two subjective forces as assigning value to gold and silver, but the durability — the relative incorruptibility — of these metals meant that they and their value were liable to outlast the commodities which they served as media of exchange, and so to possess and impart a certain epistemological reality not reducible to 'fancy and agreement' in a crudely subjective sense. With the introduction of a credit mechanism, we have already seen, the value of gold was increasingly determined by the value of paper, a far more volatile substance, which served not merely to record, but to impose upon money, trade and land, in that order, the day-to-day fluctuations of public confidence, the creature of public hopes and fears, desires and passions, themselves highly manipulable by designing and wicked men. The element of fancy, even more than that of agreement, suddenly and disastrously increased its importance. The notion of passion, which it could be used to contain, might clearly be applied to men's desire for material goods; but when the commodities to be bought and sold were paper tokens of men's confidence in their rulers and in one another, the concept of fantasy could more properly be applied, and could bear the meaning not only of illusion and imagination, but of men's opinions of others' opinions of them.

There thus grew up an epistemology of fantasy, as an inherent part of the Augustan critique of capitalism. Here, for instance, is Charles Davenant, a Tory economist, writing about 1698:

of all beings that have existence only in the minds of men, nothing is more fantastical and nice than Credit; it is never to be forced; it hangs upon opinion, it depends upon our passions of hope and fear; it comes many times unsought for, and often goes away without reason, and when once lost, is hardly to be quite recovered. It very much resembles, and, in many instances, is near akin to that fame and reputation which men obtain by wisdom in governing state affairs, or by valour and conduct in the field. An able statesman, and a great captain, may, by some ill accident, slip, or misfortune, be in disgrace, and lose the present vogue and opinion; yet this, in time, will be regained, where there is shining worth, and a real stock of merit. In the same manner, Credit, though it may be for a while obscured, and labour under some difficulties, yet it may, in some measure, recover, where there is a safe and good foundation at the bottom.

Davenant has entered upon the sociology of knowledge; he is discussing for us the epistemology of the investing society. Credit, or opinion, is the appropriate form for the ancient faculty of experience to take where money and war have speeded up the operations of society, and men must constantly translate their evaluations of the public good into actions of investment and speculation. Here, writing just after the peace of 1697, he is depicting it working in a fairly benign and reasonable way; there are conditions under which men can assay one another, and their common affairs, much as they really are, and then

men's minds will become quiet and appeased; mutual convenience will lead them into a desire of helping one another. They will find, that no trading nation ever did subsist, and carry on its business by real stock; that trust and confidence in each other, are as necessary to link and hold a people together, as obedience, love, friendship, or the intercourse of speech. And when experience has taught each man how weak he is, depending only upon himself, he will be willing to help others, and call upon the assistance of his neighbours, which of course, by degrees, must set credit again afloat.

There are the beginnings here of a civic morality of investment and exchange, but its epistemological foundations are terribly fragile. Credit 'hangs upon opinion' and 'depends upon our passions of hope and fear'; this is because the objects of its knowledge are not altogether real. It is only in part our opinions of men and things which we declare and which shape our actions, for this theory presupposes a society in which gold and paper have become the symbolic medium in which we express our feelings and translate them into actions, and have at the same time acquired a fictitious value of their own. The language in which we communicate has itself been reified and has become an object of desire, so that the knowledge and messages it conveys have been perverted and rendered less rational. And the institutions of funded debt and public stocks have turned the counters of language into marketable commodities, so that the manipulators of their value are in a position to control and falsify 'the intercourse of speech'.[12]

And here, on the other side of the political fence, is Daniel Defoe, writing about 1706 in the Whig-sponsored *Review*:

> Money has a younger Sister, a very useful and officious Servant in Trade, which in the absence of her senior Relation, but with her Consent, and on the Supposition of her Confederacy, is very assistant to her; frequently supplies her place for a Time, answers all the Ends of Trade perfectly, and to all Intents and Purposes, as well as Money herself; only with one Proviso, That her Sister constantly and punctually relieves her, keeps Time with her, and preserves her good Humour: but if she be never so little disappointed, she grows sullen, sick, and ill-natur'd, and will be gone for a great while together: Her Name in our Language is call'd CREDIT, in some Countries Honour, and in others, I know not what . . .
>
> 'Tis a strange thing to think, how absolute this Lady is; how despotickly she governs all her Actions: If you court her, you lose her, or must buy her at unreasonable Rates; and if you do, she is always jealous of you, and Suspicious; and if you don't discharge her to a Tittle of your Agreement, she is gone, and perhaps may never come again as long as you live; and if she does, 'tis with long Entreaty and abundance of Difficulty.[13]

Defoe is describing Credit in precisely the idiom employed by Machiavelli to describe *fortuna* and *occasione*. Like these Renaissance goddesses, she typifies the instability of secular things, brought about by the interactions of particular human wills, appetites and passions, and it comes as no surprise to find other passages, also written in 1706, in which she is shown operating malignantly and irrationally.

> Some give Men no Rest till they are in their Debt, and then give them no Rest till they are out again; some will credit no body, and some again are for crediting every body; some get Credit till they can pay nothing, and some break tho' they could pay all. No Nation in the World can show such mad Doings in Trade, as we do.
>
> Debtors abuse Creditors, and Creditors starve and murther their Debtors; Compassion flies from human Nature in the course of universal Commerce; and *Englishmen*, who in all other Cases are Men of Generosity, Tenderness, and more than common Compassions, are to their Debtors meer Lunaticks, Mad-men and Tyrants . . .

[12] Sir Charles Whitworth (ed.), *The Political and Commercial Works of . . . Charles D'Avenant*, London, 1771, Vol.I, pp.151-2.

[13] Daniel Defoe, *The Review*, 3(5), pp.17-18.

Is it a Mystery, that Nations should grow rich by War? that *England* can lose so many Ships by pyrating, and yet encrease? Why is War a greater Mystery than Trade, and why should Trade it self be more mysterious than in War? Why do *East India* Company's Stock rise, when Ships are taken? Mine Adventures raise Annuities, when Funds fall; lose their Vein of Oar in the Mine, and yet find it in the Shares; let no Man wonder at these Paradoxes, since such strange things are practised every Day among us?

If any Man requires an Answer to such things as these, they may find it in this Ejaculation — Great is the Power of Imagination!

Trade is a Mystery, which will never be compleatly discover'd or understood; it has its Critical Junctures and Seasons, when acted by no visible Causes, it suffers Convulsion Fitts, hysterical Disorders, and most unaccountable Emotions — Sometimes it is acted by the evil Spirit of general Vogue, and like a meer Possession 'tis hurry'd out of all manner of common Measures; today it obeys the Course of things, and submits to Causes and Consequences; tomorrow it suffers Violence from the Storms and Vapours of Human Fancy, operated by exotick Projects, and then all runs counter, the Motions are excentrick, unnatural and unaccountable — A Sort of Lunacy in Trade attends all its Circumstances, and no Man can give a rational Account of it.[14]

The motive force of the investing society, then, appeared to these Augustans as irrational fantasy and false consciousness. Not only was society now pervaded with a hysterically volatile system of perceptions and reactions; Defoe's equation of credit with honour informs us that investing men were now expected to be obsessed with what others thought, or might think of them, and this theme runs on through the sociology of Mandeville and Montesquieu — in whom 'honour' turns out to denote less any kind of feudal ethos than the nervous intersubjectivity of rentier society — to emerge in Rousseau as the distinction between *amour propre* and *amour de soi-même*. Only the individual whose personality was founded on real property could perceive himself as real and virtuous; the creature of the credit mechanism must be a creature of passion, fantasy and other-directedness.

However should the credit mechanism operate, as Davenant had indicated, so that men's perceptions of one another, and of one anothers' perceptions, were well founded, the investing society's self-image might become a perception of a real world. Here is Defoe to the same effect:

Credit is not a dependant upon the Person of the Sovereign, upon a Ministry, or upon this or that Management; but upon the Honour of

[14] Daniel Defoe, *The Review*, 3(92), p.365 and 3(126), pp.502-3.

the Publick Administration in *General*, and the Justice of *Parliaments in Particular*, in keeping whole the Interest of those that have ven-tur'd their Estates upon the Publick Faith — Nor must any *Intervention of Parties* be of Notice in this Case — For if one Party being uppermost shall refuse to make good the Deficiencies of the Ministry *that went before them*, because another Party then had the Manage-ment, *Parliamentary Credit* would be worth a Farthing . . .

Credit is too wary, too Coy a Lady to stay with any People upon such mean Conditions; if you will entertain this Virgin, you must Act upon the nice Principles of Honour, and Justice; you must preserve Sacred all the Foundations, and build regular Structures upon them; you must answer all Demands, with a respect to the solemnity, and Value of the Engagement; with respect to Justice, and Honour, and without any respect to Parties — If this is not observ'd, Credit will not come; No, tho' the Queen should call; tho' the Parliament shou'd call, or tho' the whole Nation should call.[15]

Fantasy and false consciousness could, under appropriate political conditions, be converted into men's good opinion of, and confidence in, one another, and this would be at least a move in the direction of rationality and virtue. The more capitalist man's perception could be of real goods in circulation, instead of the mere fluctuating tokens of the exchange media, the more he could perceive other men and himself as real; and this was in itself a powerful motive for depicting mercantile society as based upon trade rather than credit. Addison, in the *Spectator*, depicted the Royal Exchange, which an enemy might have seen as a hysterical throng of stockjobbers, as a concourse of solid merchants conveying real goods through the medium of real money, and the goddess Credit as collapsing into unreality at the sight of the emblems of popery and republicanism, but restored to solidity by those of Protestantism and constitutionalism.[16] But when he went on to elabo-rate a social dialogue between Sir Roger de Coverley, the country squire, and Sir Andrew Freeport, the London merchant, it is plain that Addison was playing the motherhood game again. Nobody wished to attack Sir Andrew, and everybody wished to claim him as their own; he was merely a screen for the far more compromising presences of city financiers, like Pope's Sir Balaam in his *Letter to Bathurst*, who were much more exposed to attack and much more difficult to defend. The Whig tactic was to move from credit to trade, from tokens of exchange to real com-modities, from fantasy and passion to reality and rational virtue. When what we have taken to be the classical bourgeois — rational in his cal-

[15] *The Review*, 7(116), p.463.
[16] *The Spectator*, (3, 69).

culation of real values, virtuous in his frugal avoidance of passion and prodigality — enters at this point in the role of Sir Andrew Freeport; he is to a considerable degree a debating device. I suggest that there is a real sense in which the Protestant ethic was invented by Augustan Whigs — though this does not preclude its having actually existed at an earlier time — as a means of extricating themselves from the shadow world of credit and conforming to the paradigm of virtue.

But though passion and fantasy were convertible into opinion and confidence, these latter were far more *doxa* than *episteme*. They rested upon men's perceptions of entities so shifting and subjective that they were far more likely to be the objects of passion and prejudice than rational and understanding; and Davenant and Defoe could convert fantasy into confidence only by adding experience to passion and making opinion. To construct a political system which would effect such a conversion was not easy. There is an interesting essay in Book 12, chapter 27 of the *Esprit des Lois* in which Montesquieu depicts a commercial society — obviously Britain — in which expanding wealth and personal liberty ensure that a politics of fear and avarice, faction and passion, will have the effect of converting *crédit* into *confiance*; Montesquieu is in search, more critically than Mandeville, of the sociological conditions under which 'private vices' can prove 'public benefits'. But there is a very long way to go to a strictly market politics, and it is not yet clear how, if ever, we are to arrive there.

It was notoriously difficult for passion to become *episteme* as opposed to *doxa*, and the eighteenth century's concern with constructing systems of rationality based directly upon passion clearly has much to do with an awareness that society was now based upon exchange and credit rather than on real property and personal autonomy. No exercise in Marxist demystification, incidentally, is necessary to see that — Davenant, Defoe and Addison, like Mandeville, Hume and Rousseau, are singularly explicit about what they are doing. There existed, of course, techniques — Hobbesian, Hartleian, Benthamite — for rendering the sense perceptions of the individual so specific that he could begin to calculate rationally about them; but the individual calculating about the objects of his own desires was not identical with the individual of classical humanist politics, entering into civic relationships with others equal with but unlike himself, which together with his autonomy were the conditions of his virtue and personal integrity. The individual of rational egoist theory could appeal to no paradigm of virtue comparable to this, and it was not claimed on his behalf that he could. This deficiency in individualist ideology made it difficult to maintain the thesis

that he had successfully converted his passion into reason, and where
Hobbesian and other theories of rational self-interest are found in the
age between the revolutions, they are put forward in defence of what is
sometimes called the court as opposed to the country thesis – on
behalf of a sovereign parliament, a credit mechanism and a patronage-
wielding and war-making oligarchy, which both court and country
theorists concede has moved society decisively forward, into commercial
modernity and away from a paradigm of virtue which can only be
located in an agrarian past and viewed with nostalgia. In Machiavellian
terms, rational egoism is *virtù* rather than virtue, so far as the two can
be opposed; it is the appropriate strategy for those who accept that the
movement of history is away from virtue and towards corruption, and
it is used to defend a centralised, modernising and dynamic oligarchy.
In what circumstances it became an instrument of radical attack upon
the oligarchy of Old Corruption is another story, belonging to the age
that followed the American and French Revolutions, which I do not think
we yet understand, or will understand so long as we believe that it
played that role in the eighteenth century proper.

The story I have attempted to tell is not one in which a trading
bourgeoisie, in the narrower sense of that term, was perceived as playing
a revolutionary role. Obviously such persons existed and were a necessary part of what was going on; but they were familiar actors on the
stage, and nobody considered them the dynamic or crucial element. The
revolutionary class – and Augustan social critics were in no doubt that
they were living in a revolution – was made up of soldiers, placemen,
rentiers, stockjobbers and parliamentary oligarchs – the 'monied
interest' properly defined. These were seen as making a revolutionary
impact upon the merchants and traders, whom they sharply divided
into those who had succeeded in boarding credit's bandwagon, and
those who had failed. The objection I sense to using the term 'bourgeoisie' to denote 'monied interest' is that that word, as ordinarily used,
is unduly inclusive of all kinds of entrepreneurial activity and unduly
exclusive of, or antithetical to, elements of a supposed feudalism which
was not really present. The objective phenomenon present to the
Augustan consciousness was the credit mechanism with its operators
and hangers-on; the Gothic freeman, a civic rather than a feudal type,
and the thrifty tradesman, concepts developed upon either side of it,
were abstract by comparison. The 'monied interest', however, which
was defined as revolutionary, was also defined as a class in something
like the Marxian sense: a category of persons whose power rested upon
a new mode of property and of the relations of property to the state.

What struck contemporaries about this new mode of property was not its independence of public authority, but its corrupt dependence on government, which tended to convert public authority into a private interest.

The Augustan version of radical democracy was intended for those, operating whoever they were under an agrarian paradigm, who felt their autonomy and virtue threatened by the manipulative state that went with the credit mechanism. Since we know now that the ideology which opposed virtue to corruption was an important force in bringing about the revolt of the American colonies,[17] we can say that it was an ideology capable of operating in a revolutionary sense. But such a revolution would not perceive itself simply as an enlightened or rational revolt against a traditional past. It must also adopt the language and style of a revolt against modernity. Since no alternative had yet been found for a paradigm of virtue that presupposed an unspecialised and agrarian individualism, best anchored in real property and a pre-commercial past, both mainstreams of thought — Whigs and Tories, Hamiltonians and Jeffersonians — were obliged to presume that the movement of history was away from value and towards amoral and irrational change. This made their thinking a vitally important link between Renaissance theories of cyclical degeneration and Romantic theories of historical dialectic. If I do not consider that the story I have been telling is compatible with conventional Marxism, and so that I have not been performing as a Marxist historian, I do consider that I have been doing a piece of the history of Marxism. Around 1698 was when it all began, and some of its roots were in civic humanism. But just when, if ever, a classical bourgeois ideology and a market theory of personality came to hold possession of the field, my researches have yet to reveal to me.

[17] Bernard Bailyn, *The Ideological Origins of the American Revolution*, Cambridge, Mass., 1967; Gordon S. Wood, *The Creation of the American Republic, 1776-1787*, Chapel Hill, 1969; Gerald Stourzh, *Alexander Hamilton and the Idea of Republican Government*, Stanford, 1970; J. G. A. Pocock, 'Virtue and Commerce in the Eighteenth Century', *Journal of Interdisciplinary History*, 1972.

4

'The Bourgeoisie, Historically, has played a Most Revolutionary Part'

R. S. Neale

I have chosen as my text the sentence from the *Communist Manifesto*, 'The bourgeoisie, historically, has played a most revolutionary part',[1] and my reason for attempting to approach our subject in this indirect way is to try to avoid the dangers of reification inherent in all discussions of feudalism, traditional society, capitalism, industrialism, and so on and to remind us, as Marx frequently did his contemporaries, that capital and capitalism necessarily imply the existence of a human capitalist — a bourgeois. But, when I came to put my thoughts in order, there seemed to be as much difficulty with the term bourgeoisie as with the concept capitalism. Works of reference were no help. The 1971 edition of the *Encyclopaedia of the Social Sciences* is very abrupt. Under bourgeoisie it says, 'In Great Britain and the U.S. bourgeoisie had nearly disappeared from the vocabulary of political writers and politicians by the mid twentieth century.' This is in contrast to the *Encyclopaedia Britannica* of sixty years earlier which was confident that the bourgeoisie was 'the trading middle class of any country'. It is also in contrast to the usage of historians. There can be very few commentators on modern English history who do not use the term bourgeoisie even if only to point out that before the mid-nineteenth century England never had one and that there is no English word to describe the concept. Others use it implicitly when they endorse or oppose the validity of the notion of the embourgeoisement of the working class. However, most historians, even Marxist ones, use the term as a synonym for middle class or, as I have already done, for a class of capitalists. For example Book 2 of Morazé's *The Triumph of the Middle Classes* (original title *Les Bourgeois Conquérants*) is called *The Bourgeois Revolution 1780-*

[1] K. Marx and F. Engels, *Selected Works*, 3 vols., Moscow, 1969, Vol.1, p.111.

1840 and it has a sub-section on England called 'The Middle Classes Take Over'. E. J. Hobsbawm, too, moves easily between several terms to express this single concept. According to these and other historians the 'bourgeoisie' was *the* dynamic group leading the development of the modern world. Further, when bourgeois is used as an adjective as in 'bourgeois ideology' we tend to nod sagely as if we all understand and agree on what this ideology is and that what it is can be, perhaps must be, exclusively attributed and attached to the bourgeoisie.

Now, although we might press historians to choose their words with care and to formulate, with greater verbal precision, any explanatory apparatus they might use, we are unlikely to meet with much success, at least in the short term. So, in order to get closer to the concept beneath the words I would like to highlight what the Marx of the *Communist Manifesto* had to say in elaboration of the text with which I started. Marx recognised that the bourgeoisie he eulogised was 'itself the product of a long course of development, of a series of revolutions in the modes of production and of exchange'[2] and that it had taken a variety of forms in the process of its evolution until 'the place of manufacture was taken by the giant, Modern Industry, the place of the industrial middle class, *by industrial millionaires, the leaders of whole industrial armies, the modern bourgeois*'.[3] It seems that what Marx meant by bourgeois was the modern bourgeois about 1850, the big (millionaire) industrial bourgeois and, according to *Capital*, a bourgeois for whom 'the increasing appropriation of abstract wealth is the sole motive of his operation'.[4] This was the revolutionary bourgeoisie which in less than 100 years, from about 1750, 'has created more massive and more colossal productive forces than have all preceding generations together'.[5] Yet, as Marx agrees, this bourgeoisie was itself a result as well as a cause of this expansion. The paradox is only partially resolved by praxis, the big bourgeoisie was not its own product. In Marx's own model big bourgeois came from little ones but little ones grew from serfs who created towns anew with the break-up of feudalism consequent on the growth of markets and world trade, that is they were new men outside the agricultural sector.

In this *Communist Manifesto, German Ideology* model of Marxist

[2] Ibid., p.110.

[3] Ibid., p.110. My italics. For a discussion of the origin of the term see Shirley Gruner, 'The Revolution of July 1830 and the Expression "Bourgeoisie" ', *Historical Journal*, 11 (3), 1968. For the symbolism in Marx's usage see Robert Tucker, *Philosophy and Myth in Karl Marx*, Cambridge, 1961.

[4] *Capital*, Everyman ed., p.138.

[5] K. Marx and F. Engels, *Selected Works*, Vol.1, p.113.

history it appears that men can only make or transform themselves out-side the rural sector and in response to exogenous forces, in this case the extrusion of serfs and, in particular, the growth of international trade following the discovery of the Americas and the rounding of the Cape. At the heart of this model lies the notion that the pre-industrial agri-cultural societies of western Europe, whatever one chooses to call them, could not change themselves without the emergence of a sector and a class outside the agricultural one. As Sweezy said in a review of Dobb's alternative Marxist model, 'Dobb has not succeeded in shaking that part of the commonly accepted theory which holds that the root cause of the decline of feudalism was the growth of trade'.[6]

Behind *this* notion of the rigidity of agricultural societies there lies the nineteenth-century bourgeois antagonism to conservative agricul-turalists and powerful landowning aristocracies. Marx frequently com-mented on the antagonism between town and country and considered it a necessary condition for the separation of capital from landed property, that is, as 'the beginning of property having its basis only in labour and exchange'[7] without which capitalism could not be said to exist. In the *Grundrisse*, for example, he comments that 'it was a great step forward when the industrial or commercial system came to see the source of wealth not in the object but in the activity of persons, viz. in commercial and industrial labour'. Marx also praised the physiocratic system as a further step forward since it considered a certain form of labour, namely agricultural labour, as the source of wealth, not in the disguise of money, but as 'product in general'. Nevertheless, according to Marx, this physio-cratic view was still a limited one. The 'product in general' was still only a natural product and land was regarded as the source of production par excellence. Marx then went on to say:

> It was a tremendous advance on the part of Adam Smith to throw aside all the limitations which mark wealth-producing activity and to define it as labour in general, neither industrial nor commercial nor agricultural, or one as much as the other. Along with the universal character of wealth-creating activity we now have the universal character of the object defined as wealth, viz. product in general, or labour in general, but as past, objectified labour.

That is, Capital. Marx went on to say: *'How difficult and how great was the transition is evident from the way Adam Smith himself falls back*

[6] P. M. Sweezy, M. Dobb et al., *The Transition from Feudalism to Capitalism*, New York, 1963, p.7.

[7] K. Marx and F. Engels, *The German Ideology*, Moscow, 1968, p.66.

from time to time into the physiocratic system'.[8] As far as I know, Marx, unlike Ricardo, never committed this physiocratic error and always attacked those bourgeois theorists who were inclined to slip back into physiocratic-type arguments. Consequently he was critical of the pessimism of Malthus as well as the optimism of the systematic colonisers. For Marx the key to productivity and the forward movement of the economy was always capital and capital accumulation, and all capital was objectified labour. It is true that Marx, in discussing primary accumulation in *Capital*, regarded the early development of capitalist agriculture in Britain as important. It was a major factor creating wage labour and supplying labour to the developing manufacturing sector. Further, it provided a market for manufactured goods and was a source of primary funds necessary to set labour to work in manufacturing. Nevertheless, according to Marx, there was a continuing tendency for peasant agriculture to re-establish itself such that capitalist agriculture could not develop and solidify into a capitalist mode of production without the prior development of industrial capitalism, 'Not until large-scale industry, based on machinery, comes, does there arise a permanent foundation for capitalist agriculture'.[9] Thus the principal human agents or mediators remained the capitalists – the big industrial bourgeois of the *Communist Manifesto*.

It seems that one of the components of Marx's concept of capitalism and of the revolutionary role he attributed to the bourgeoisie was his critique of the ideas of the physiocrats and the class for whom they spoke. Another was a conviction, shared with the eighteenth-century historians of civil or bourgeois society, that the bourgeoisie was necessarily progressive. A corollary of this was that although he considered the economic and social structure of western Europe to constitute a progressive mode of production he was also caught up in the belief that the agricultural 'feudal' societies of that part of the world could not have changed without the development of the bourgeoisie – men, perhaps, of his own kind. Certainly the greater their achievement, the greater would

[8] All extracts are from David McLellan, *Marx's Grundrisse*, London, 1971, pp.37-8. My italics.

[9] *Capital*, Everyman ed., Vol.2, p.830. However in *The Grundrisse*, Pelican Marx Library, 1973, pp.252-3, Marx wrote, 'It is, therefore, precisely in the development of landed property that the gradual victory and formation of capital can be studied . . . The history of landed property, which would demonstrate the gradual transformation of the feudal landlord into the landowner, of the hereditary, semi-tributary and often unfree tenant for life into the modern farmer, and of the resident serfs, bondsmen and villeins who belonged to the property into agricultural day-labourers, would indeed be the history of the formation of modern capital.'

be the final achievement of the proletariat; they would be giant-killers indeed fully entitled to hail the emancipation of man, 'by the crowing of the Gallic cock'. Marx, deriving his 'model' from his Prussian experience in the second quarter of the nineteenth century, was led to formulate a latecomers growth model. In it massive capital accumulation was regarded as central to the problem of economic and social change as well as the key to the proletarian emancipation of society. Such massive capital accumulation appeared impossible of achievement within the agricultural sectors of early nineteenth-century Prussia. Hence the need for a new sector and new men. Marx then applied this 'model' in an attempt to explain the first successful case of industrialisation and the actual experience of England.

I think it true to say that, since then, similar notions have for long been implicit and generally explicit in western bourgeois thought. For example, they can be found in one form or another in the work of thinkers as different in time and place as Weber and Hirschman and they are all certainly implicit if not explicit in the work of many modern economic historians. Thus, W. W. Rostow in his anti-communist-manifesto growth model[10] defines traditional society, the equivalent of Marx's feudalism, as incapable of change and postulates the need for exogenous shocks to terminate each of its first two stages: 'traditional society' and 'pre-conditions for take-off'. He also emphasises the crucial importance of a sharp upward shift in investment preceded or accompanied by the emergence of a new entrepreneurial and political élite. In this connection the most recent survey of the role of capital in the industrial revolution, that by Crouzet,[11] takes to task those economic historians who, in the recent past, have argued that capital and enterprise were derived from all sectors and sections of English society and that entrepreneurs were not a class (that is bourgeois) but a type. Although Crouzet recognises that the capital requirements in England during the period of industrialisation were relatively slight he argues that the evidence does show that there was an increase in accumulation and that the main providers of capital for productive, that is factory, investment were first the industrialists themselves and second those engaged in commerce. On the other hand he considers the part played in industrialisation by landed capital and landowners to have been 'very small'. The point is that recent work in economic history appears to give some support to the notion that industrialisation was mainly the work of newcomers,

[10] W. W. Rostow, *The Stages of Economic Growth*, Cambridge, 1960.

[11] François Crouzet, *Capital Formation in the Industrial Revolution*, London, 1972.

whether one calls them bourgeois or not. However, unless we are prepared to equate these small industrial and commercial investors, adding perhaps 1-2 per cent of national income to investment in the industrial sector from the 1780s, with the Marxist bourgeoisie, the question of the revolutionary role of the bourgeoisie during the crucial period of industrialisation in the eighteenth and early nineteenth century must remain an open and two-part one. The first question is whether a bourgeoisie as envisaged by Marx had an objective existence as a class in itself. The second is, did it exist as a class for itself? As a class for itself it certainly did not exist. English industrial capitalists or entrepreneurs (we must call them something) were either too busy making their economic fortunes, or spending them to gain entrée to the landowning and aristocratic class, to be conscious of themselves as a class in opposition to their rulers. As a class in itself it is also unlikely that it existed. It is true that there was a variety of small capitalists in the trading, manufacturing and industrial sectors in the economy, in civil society, but as yet they were only an embryonic bourgeoisie — they were certainly not the big industrial millionaires identified by Marx. On the other hand really great wealth, and the power which went with it, was still landed wealth supplemented by wealth derived from government office and financial speculation for capital gains rather than for productive purposes. For example, the wealthiest man in mid-eighteenth-century England was the first Earl of Bath who is reputed to have left a fortune of £1.6 million in 1764 and who, in 1737, opposed a reduction in the interest on the national debt because his wife's very considerable fortune was invested in government stock. Then there was the Duke of Chandos. Between 1705 and 1713 the Duke made £600,000 out of the office of paymaster at a time when only four of London's aldermen, after a lifetime of effort, possessed wealth estimated at over a quarter of a million pounds.[12] (Perhaps one question we might discuss is whether a bourgeoisie came into existence in England and if so, when?).

According to Harold Perkin, a very recent commentator on the modernisation of England, it was landed wealth and landowner consumption as well as aristocratic land-based power which provided the key to the modernisation of Britain in the eighteenth and early nineteenth centuries rather than any activity by a bourgeoisie. Moreover, according to J. H. Plumb, this landed aristocracy increased its grip on power during the period of industrialisation in the eighteenth century, while

[12] Richard Grassby, 'The Personal Wealth of the Business Community in Seventeenth-Century England', *English Historical Review*, Second Series, 23(2), August 1970.

according to Perkin and Neale, there was little or no pressure from the big bourgeoisie to challenge that power. According to Neale the politically revolutionary force in the early nineteenth century was neither a Marxist bourgeoisie nor a proletariat, but a middling class. Perhaps I might emphasise that there seems to be little doubt that the major component in the radical movements of the eighteenth and early nineteenth centuries was a sense of loss of liberties and political rights; consequently these movements were pervaded by a strongly anti-aristocratic rather than anti-bourgeois bias. The fact that at the end of the seventeenth century 4.7 per cent of the population exercised a franchise, compared with only 4.2 per cent after the 1832 Reform Bill shows that there were real rather than imagined grounds for radical opposition to the increasing power of the aristocracy throughout the eighteenth century. Guttsman has also demonstrated beyond all doubt that the landowning aristocracy retained a virtual monopoly of political power throughout most of the nineteenth century in England and many historians find no difficulty in accepting the fact that the anti-corn law league was more symptomatic of the failure of the bourgeois challenge to aristocratic power than of a bourgeois political maturity.[13] So much then for the negative aspect of my argument. But who should replace the bourgeoisie?

Earlier in this paper I referred to Dobb's alternative Marxist model and I would like now to say a little more about it as a preliminary to putting forward a model of eighteenth-century industrialisation which relegates the embryonic bourgeoisie to a minor role in relation to the more important part played by landowners, the agricultural sector and the aristocracy. First of all consider what Dobb had to say.

> Regarding the 'conservative and change resisting character of Western European feudalism', which needed some external force to dislodge it, and which I am accused of neglecting, I remain rather sceptical. True, of course, that, by contrast with a capitalist economy, feudal society was extremely stable and inert. But this is not to say that feudalism has no tendency within it to change. To say so would be to make it an exception to the general Marxist law of development that economic society is moved by its own internal contradictions.

[13] Harold Perkin, *The Origins of Modern English Society, 1780-1880*, London, 1969; J. H. Plumb, 'The Growth of the Electorate in England from 1600-1715', *Past and Present*, 45, November 1969; R. S. Neale, *Class and Ideology in the Nineteenth Century*, London, 1972; W. L. Guttsman, *The British Political Elite*, London, 1963; Carl B. Cone, *The English Jacobins*, London, 1968. See also the work of D. C. Moore, 'Concession or Cure: The Sociological Premises of the First Reform Act', *Historical Journal*, 9(1), 1966; 'Social Structure, Political Structure and Public Opinion in Mid-Victorian England', in R. Robson (ed.), *Ideas and Institutions of Victorian Britain*, London, 1967; and 'The First Reform Act: A Discussion', *Victorian Studies*, 14(3), 1971.

Actually, the feudal period witnessed considerable changes in technique; and the later centuries of feudalism showed marked differences from those of early feudalism. Sweezy qualifies his statement by saying that the feudal system is not necessarily static. All he claims is that such movement as occurs 'has no tendency to transform it'. But despite this qualification, the implication remains that under feudalism class struggle can play no revolutionary role. It occurs to me that there may be a confusion at the root of this denial of revolutionary and transforming tendencies. *No one is suggesting that class struggle of peasants against lords gives rise, in any simple and direct way, to capitalism. What this does is to modify the dependence of the petty mode of production upon the feudal overlordship and eventually to shake loose the small producer from feudal exploitation. It is then from the petty mode of production (in a degree to which it secures independence of action, and social differentiation in turn develops within it) that capitalism is born. This is a fundamental point to which we shall return.*[14]

The essence of Dobb's view, as it is of the Marxist approach to history, is that economic society is moved by its own internal contradictions, consequently exogenous factors and a prior creation of a new élite (bourgeoisie) were not necessary for the emergence of capitalism.

What Dobb argues and what a good deal of recent research shows is that because of various peculiarities in English agriculture and society *capitalism and capitalists developed within the rural sector.* Certainly recent work has shown that by the early sixteenth century English agriculture was largely a specialised and market-orientated agriculture, literally dominated in parts of the west country by large-scale capitalist farming. Over the next 200 years the agricultural sector — by far the largest sector in the economy and the source of the bulk of wealth — experienced a series of changes mostly generated in response to developments internal to that sector, although by this time there were close interconnections between the urban and the rural sectors of the economy and society. The changes I have in mind were legal, organisational, and technological. First, in the sixteenth century there was the legal shift from copyhold to leasehold, and the parallel and continuing shift from long leases for life to leases for short terms of years, both of which developments accompanied the growth of the large landed estate. Organisationally there was the consolidation of holdings, achieved largely through enclosure by agreement. Technologically the most important development was the introduction and spread of convertible husbandry from the 1560s to the mid-eighteenth century. It is a further

---

[14] Sweezy, Dobb et al., *Transition*, pp. 22-3. My italics.

pointer to the degree to which commercial attitudes and the production of exchange values had penetrated English agriculture that the practice of convertible husbandry was not dependent on the spread of enclosure but was easily and readily introduced into open field farming.[15]

This technological change was itself contingent upon the commercialisation of agriculture and, in conjunction with the relative stagnation of population growth at the end of the century, was both cause and effect of a fall in agricultural prices. This price decline increased the real incomes of those outside the agricultural sector. At this point the landowner class made a significant, albeit unconscious, contribution to the maintenance of demand by keeping up farm incomes through accepting widespread defaults in rents and pumping into agriculture income earned elsewhere in the economy. As Perkin has noted, they also increased their own consumption expenditures and created conditions favourable to consumer emulation. The biggest and clearest surviving example of the consequences of these expenditures is the city of Bath. This was built in a matter of seventy years at a total capital cost of some £2 million, an amount roughly equivalent to the fixed capital invested in the cotton industry by the end of the eighteenth century. But landowners and the aristocracy did more than consume, they also invested in crucial sectors. They invested widely in mineral extraction, timber production, and iron manufacture, and they made the bulk of investment in the turnpike system, contributed about one-third of the investment in canal construction, and played a vital role in all the urban developments of the eighteenth century. Above all, perhaps, they subscribed to the funds and then taxed themselves to build and maintain a navy which, in a militarily competitive world, was a piece of infrastructure without which the one or two per cent of national income invested in the industrial sector could never have paid off. Further, the landowner-dominated parliament and county administrations were responsible for legislative and administrative decisions which encouraged the expansion of the small industrial sector; they strove to protect wool and effectively protected cotton, they maintained the navigation laws and allowed a great range of restrictive practices to fall into disuse. They made possible the enclosure acts and invested heavily in enclosure itself. In doing so they made a contribution to increasing agricultural output without which the recurring bread riots of the eighteenth century could have turned

[15] Joan Thirsk (ed.), *The Agrarian History of England and Wales*, Vol.IV, 1500-1640, Cambridge, 1967; Eric Kerridge, *The Agricultural Revolution*, London, 1967; E. L. Jones, *Agriculture and Economic Growth in England 1650-1815*, London, 1967.

into revolution, and, insofar as they shared in the 'moral economy' of the eighteenth century, they also contributed to reducing the sharpness of the impact of market conditions.[16]

It is in this long, slowly moving history of the agricultural sector that one can see how the small producer was shaken free from direct exploitation as a serf, how nominally free labour and the petty mode of production generated capitalistic modes of production within the agricultural sector itself without the need for or example of even the embryonic bourgeoisie and long before the coming into existence of the big bourgeoisie of the *Communist Manifesto*. I think that what we need to understand about the actual growth of capitalism and the process of industrialisation, in England in particular, is that the English landowner and capitalist farmer experienced a substantial dose of embourgeoisement well before the bourgeoisie existed and before the emergence of the concept, at least as Marx envisaged it.

What I have argued so far is that landowners and the landed aristocracy, within a commercialised agricultural sector, led the transformation of England in the eighteenth century. Since it was they who wielded political, economic, and social power it is inconceivable, in the absence of revolution, that the case could have been in any way different. I have denied that the variety of small investors and capitalists in civil society were a class or that they constituted a bourgeoisie in Marx's sense. I have described the landowning class as having experienced a degree of embourgeoisement. In much of what I have said I am in full agreement with Harold Perkin in his *The Origin of Modern English Society*. But I wish now to press the argument further and to consider the extent to which the changing needs of landowners led to significant changes in law and institutions and the manner in which this changing law was also a necessary pre-condition for the development of a capitalist society and for the industrialisation of England, as well as being a precondition for the clarification of notions of capital without which the concept of capitalism itself could not have emerged.

When historians make their rare comments on relationships between law, the economic transformation of England and the growth of capitalism, they generally do so from only one point of view: that of the contribution of law to the development of economic liberalism. They

[16] Some of the sources for these views are to be found in: Perkin, *Modern English Society*; William Albert, *The Turnpike Road System in England 1663-1840*, Cambridge, 1972; Crouzet, *Capital Formation*; G. E. Mingay, *English Landed Society in the Eighteenth Century*, London, 1963; J. T. Ward and R. G. Wilson, *Land and Industry*, London, 1971; C. W. Chalklin, 'Urban Housing Estates in the Eighteenth Century', *Urban Studies*, 5(1), February 1968.

discuss Davenant v. Hurdis and D'Arcy v. Allein to point out how the
one effectively challenged the monopolist powers of corporate bodies
and the other the powers of the crown. They might also consider the
Statute of Monopolies, mention the Bubble Act, and look at the falling
into disuse and eventual repeal of a mass of restrictive legislation. More
sophisticated versions, like that of Harold Perkin, will interpret Locke
in order to emphasise the emergence, at the end of the seventeenth
century, of a concept of absolute private property.[17] However, although
property is clearly a matter for the courts, Perkin and others have not
discussed concepts of property in connection with any legal decisions
in regard to land or property. Yet I would expect an examination of
land law and property law to reveal more about the beliefs and attitudes
of society in respect to property than the writings of more well known
polemicists.

I do not wish to underestimate the importance of economic liberalism
or the development of a concept of absolute private property for the
central problem of this symposium or for the emergence of capitalism.
Insofar as they facilitated the shaking loose of the petty producer and
the property owner from collectivist restraints they did make a contribution to the transformation of England. However, to set producers
and property owners 'free' as compulsorily independent agents and then
to endow them with a concept of private property as something 'absolute, categorical and unconditional' could have produced a legal and
conceptual framework for a merely fragmented society of petty producers, that is while setting producers free these developments do not
make it legally possible for them to do anything much with that freedom. I would therefore like to look at some aspects of the development
of land and property law in order to show two things. First, that a
property law, which embodied and projected a concept of property as
something increasingly flexible and functional rather than absolute and
categorical, had developed in England by the second half of the seventeenth century and had developed out of the changing demands of the
class of landowners rather than out of the needs or because of the
ideology of a bourgeoisie. Second, that it was this aristocratic/land-
owning property law and concept of property which provided the legal
and a good deal of the institutional framework which alone made possible the development of industrial capitalism in England. If I can make
good this claim then it seems to me that one can fairly say that not only
was the bourgeoisie not its own product but that it really was the

[17]Perkin, *Modern English Society*, pp.51-3; C. B. Macpherson, *The Political
Theory of Possessive Individualism*, Oxford, 1962.

creature of the aristocracy — a sort of Balfour's Poodle in reverse!

The first thing that has to be said about land law in England after the conquest is that it was centrally administered and relatively uncomplicated, there were no allods as on the continent and all land was held on tenure, that is by contract.[18] Neither common law nor equity recognised absolute titles. The next thing that has to be said is that almost from the very beginning (after the conquest) property was inheritable and lords sought powers to alienate freely and at will mainly to avoid the heavy burden of feudal incidents and to found a dynasty. This led to a development in law which was peculiarly English, the use. This effectively divided property between the trustees with seisin and the beneficiary or *cestui que use.* Here already was a sophisticated breakdown of rights in property in land; the crown had some rights, the grantor and trustees others, and the *cestui que use* yet others. As a consequence there was a continuing struggle between all interested parties highlighted in the modern period by the Statute of Uses, 1535-6, and the problems which it produced. By not executing all uses this statute recognised some uses but, for the most part, turned use into possession. Subsequently the Statute of Wills, 1540, reversed some of the conditions of the Statute of Uses and compounded further the problem of clarifying titles to land. The main battleground was Chancery and so hard fought was the battle that by the mid-seventeenth century uncertainty about who held legal title was such that Lord Chief Justice Hale, after a purchase of land, is reported to have said that he would gladly pay another year's purchase in order to be sure of his title! Much of the ground for uncertainty about title was removed with the final abolition of military tenures and the abolition of the crown's prerogatives in regard to land in 1660. But, even though landowners had secured their titles against the claims of the crown, and, through their attack on customary tenures, copyholds and long-lifehold leases, against the

---

[18] The following comments on law are based on work on several hundred leases, building leases, conveyances and mortgages in the Guildhall Archives of the City of Bath and the Somerset County Record Office, Taunton and on the work of legal historians: Sir William Holdsworth, *Historical Introduction to the Land Law*, and *A History of English Law*; A. W. B. Simpson, *An Introduction to the History of Land Law*, Oxford, 1961; D. E. C. Yale, *Lord Nottingham's Chancery Cases*, Selden Society, London, 1961; E. W. Ives, 'The Genesis of the Statute of Uses', *English Historical Review*, 82(325), October 1967; Mary Cotterell, 'Interregnum Law Reform: The Hale Commission of 1652', *English Historical Review*, 83, October 1968 and private communication on the Hale Commission; B. Coward, 'Disputed Inheritances: Some Difficulties of the Nobility in the late Sixteenth and early Seventeenth Centuries', *Bulletin of the Institute of Historical Research*, 44, November 1971. See also Wolfgang Friedmann, *Law in a Changing Society*, 2nd ed., London, 1972, pp.93-101.

claims of the peasantry, the use in the form of the settlement persisted
with the result that virtually every nominal landowner had only qualified
title to property. In fact the secret of the classic settlement was to turn
every possessor into a life tenant. This device contributed greatly to
clarifying and consolidating titles but it also placed severe restrictions
on the freedom of action of the possessor. As a result of these developments, by the last quarter of the seventeenth century the courts recognised at least three types of rights or powers in landed property: the
rights of the original devisor or grantor of an estate; the rights of the
trustees appointed by him; and the rights of the beneficiary. With the
growth of the mortgage and the elaboration of equity of redemption,
both of which were by-products of the stability of the settled estate, the
courts recognised a fourth right, that of mortgagees and their executors
to a share in the income from land. As landowners developed their
lands, for example, when building was carried out on leasehold land at
Bath, rights in land and property became even more divided; landlords
retained rights to fee farm rents but developers gained rights to ground
rents and builders to house rents, and all had powers to sell or mortgage
their respective rights but only without detriment to the property rights
of the others.

The rights of beneficiaries, and the claims arising from ground rents
are interesting since in neither instance was there any absolute right to
property as an object, that is land, only legal titles to the money income
from property. As mortgages developed, following the elaboration of
rules in regard to equity of redemption by Lord Nottingham in the
1670s, and although they could only ensure rights to income and not
to land, they began to take on many of the characteristics of property.
As Lord Hardwicke put it in 1738,

> An equity of redemption is considered as an estate in land; it will
> descend, may be granted, devised, entailed, and that equitable estate
> may be barred by a common recovery. This proves that it is not con-
> sidered as a mere right, but as such an estate, whereof, in the considera-
> tion of this court, there may be a seisin for without such a seisin, a
> devise could not be good.[19]

Since ground rents could be mortgaged as well as sold it is clear that the
law had arrived at a very sophisticated and flexible concept of property
at least as early as 1700. My own recent work on building in the city of
Bath in the eighteenth century leaves me in no doubt that this concept
of property was part of popular culture and I would go so far as to say

[19] Simpson, *History of Land Law*, p.228.

that the great achievement of the developers of Bath depended upon this fact. It is also worth noting that titles to ground rents and building mortgages represented titles to exchange values (property) arising from the application of labour and/or capital (objectified labour) to land.

Thus, whatever the notions in regard to property held by economic and political theorists at the turn of the seventeenth and eighteenth centuries, society and the law recognised the divisibility of property titles and recognised legal titles to present and future income as property, thus giving legal form to the notion that property was the product of labour and capital as well as the product of land and of all three together. Other paper titles that, like mortgages, were regarded as property in the early eighteenth century were bills of exchange. While the importance of the bill of exchange for the finance of a vast range of transactions and thereby for the financing of industry is now generally recognised, the importance of the mortgage on land for similar purposes is now only being discovered. It is also worth noting that the courts permitted penalty rates on unpaid interest and made it possible to charge a little more than the legal maximum. All these developments flowed from the changing needs of landowners, and they point to the existence of a world in which credit, like the English weather, was a fact of life — credit was property.

Further, the Lockian notion that property meant freedom to use to the extent of destroying[20] was not applicable to landed property. Titles to land were so intermixed with the titles of others that few property owners had anything approaching that kind of power. The restrictions on life tenants on settled estates have already been alluded to but even land held in fee simple rarely gave the possessor absolute title or power. But the last word on this should be allowed to the lawyer author of *Tenants Law* who, with a wealth of experience and judgment of men, wrote:

> A man that is seized in land or tenements to hold to him and his heirs forever, is said to be tenant in fee simple; and such an estate is called Feodum Simplex. And indeed fee simple is the most pure holding; that is, being unmixed or intangled in itself. But as the whitest colour will soon be tainted, so is this pure tenure most subject to be spotted and involved in troubles above any other; which the law calls incumbrances.
>
> If a man was to deal as purchaser with a tenant in fee simple, he hath a happy bargain if he meets with a simple tenure and a simple tenant; I mean the one free from incumbrances, and the other from

[20] John Locke, *Two Treatises of Government*, Cambridge, 1963, p.203.

deceit; which many have found it a difficult thing to obtain.

I shall therefore, by way of caution, set down the several troubles and incumbrances this pure tenure, called fee simple is subject unto.

Fee simple may be incumbered with several judgements, statutes merchant, and of the staple, recognizances, mortgages, wills, precontracts, bargains and sales, feoffments, fines, amerciament, jointures, dowers, and many other feudal conveyances if a knave once possess it; and last of all, may be quite forfeited for treason, or felony which incurs forfeitures.

But fee simple being free from any of the above mentioned incumbrances, is the most free, absolute and ample estate of inheritance that any man can have; and therefore a tenant in fee simple is said to be seized in his domain as of fee.[21]

Thus, whatever the state of theory about property, the law and society worked with a fee simple tenure so spotted that the quantity of spots changed the quality of the beast. As the Duke of Portland discovered in 1767 the beast could be a very nasty one. What he had believed to be a grant of land in fee simple from the crown was, according to his political enemies, an estate tail which the crown had no powers to alienate. His estate in the Forest of Inglewood was resumed by the crown and granted to Sir James Lowther.[22]

So to the second point I wish to make. The key to most of these encumbrances, as it was also the key to the flexibility of property law, was the use or the trust which seems to me to have been also the legal embodiment of the moral position that the liberty of the propertyowner ought to be circumscribed by familial and dynastic considerations as well as by the legitimate claims of others. The trust, according to Holdsworth, has

> played a part in the development of our public law, larger and more direct than that played by contract. They (trusts) have peopled our state with groups and associations which have enabled the individual persons who have created or have composed them to accomplish much more than any single individual composing them could have accomplished.

This was also Maitland's opinion: 'If I were asked', he said, 'what is the greatest and most distinctive achievement performed by Englishmen in the field of jurisprudence I cannot think that we should have any better

[21] *Tenants Law*, 17th ed., London, 1777, p.4.

[22] James Adair, *Observations on the Power of the Crown*, London, 1767.

answer than this; namely the development from century to century of the trust idea'.[23]

As I have already argued, these trusts grew out of the dynastic ambition of landowners and out of their struggle with the crown for the right to alienate freely — a right fully achieved only in 1660. The paradox was that while each landowner sought the right to alienate for himself he sought it with the purpose of denying it to his heirs, hence the great growth of the trust and the settled estate particularly after the work of a number of eminent conveyancers like Sir Orlando Bridgman at the end of the seventeenth century. By the early eighteenth century many of these settled estates functioned like joint stock companies; through the creation of life tenancies ownership was distinguished from management and use, the claims of investors (mortgagees) were given preferences, while the claims of all beneficiaries put pressures on salaried estate managers and agents to maximise the income from the undertaking. Any policy changes had to be discussed by what was in fact a board of trustees. When the issue was a complex one recourse had to be made to parliament to alter the terms of the settlement by statute for only in this way could the restrictions on life tenants be removed — there is increasing evidence to show that enterprising landowners did seek new powers. For example, William Johnstone Pulteney, husband of the heir of the Earl of Bath, persuaded the trustees of his wife's estate in Bathwick, near Bath, to secure an act of parliament in 1769 to permit the exploitation of that estate for building development. Under the act the number of trustees was increased to four and they were given powers to: build a bridge (to link Bathwick with Bath), raise £3000 on mortgage, grant ninety-nine year building leases, buy or exchange land with any corporate body, convey three springs of water to Bath, and charge all costs to the estate. The bridge-building project proved more costly than was envisaged and made it necessary to obtain two more acts of parliament to raise mortgages to finance a total investment of £11,000. By the end of the century, however, this initial investment had made possible a further £300,000 investment in real estate and produced an estimated threefold increase in income to the family.[24]

As legal historians are aware, the trust was adapted to a variety of purposes. It was, for example, the legal instrument which enabled 'bourgeois' dissenting groups to hold property and build meeting

[23] W. Holdsworth, *A History of English Law*, 3rd ed., London, 1945, Vol.IV, pp.407-80 (quote p.408); F. W. Maitland, 'Trust and Corporation', *Collected Papers*, London, 1911, Vol.III, pp.356-403.

[24] Based on the Pulteney Estate Papers deposited in Bath Reference Library.

houses. It provided the legal basis for the turnpike trust which in 1706 began to replace the old justice trust. It is also worth noting that the earliest of the turnpike trusts were all in rich agricultural areas while the fourth of them, in 1707, was the Bath Trust, designed to facilitate the flow of wealthy and largely aristocratic consumers to what was described as 'a valley of pleasure and a sink of iniquity'. The trust, in the form of the equitable trust, has also been traced in financing the fulling, brass, insurance, flour-milling and building industries as well as in the big American land companies in the eighteenth century. It was a form of financial organisation which made possible what the Bubble Act expressly prohibited. In the most developed trusts the trust had a cor-porate existence, ownership was separated from management, there was limited liability and transferability and sale of shares. Indeed, in the course of the eighteenth century limited liability came to be written into the policies of unincorporated insurance companies, thereby demonstrating the degree of public confidence in the trust form.[25] It is worth remembering that the trust developed in response to the needs and as a result of the power of landowners — the embryonic bourge-oisie of the eighteenth century merely borrowed it almost intact. Further, since the analogies we use reflect our own perception of the world, we would do well to consider the possibility that when Locke wrote his *Two Treatises of Government* he might have had the image of a settled estate or trust in mind rather than that of a joint stock com-pany. To change the analogies we use is to alter the concept we wish to express.

I began with the text 'The bourgeoisie, historically, has played a most revolutionary part' and I have ended with the notion that what passed for a bourgeoisie in the period preceding the most rapid trans-formation in eighteenth-century England was more caused by than cause of that transformation. On the other hand I have sought to emphasise the 'revolutionary' role of landowners and the aristocracy, in regard to not only their objective contribution to things like industrial investment, agricultural improvement, urban development, and con-sumption, but also their crucial contribution to developing an ideology, law and institutions favourable to that transformation. The basic point I wish to make is that the landowning and political élite in England — like the later bourgeoisie and proletariat — also made and changed

[25] C. A. Cooke, *Corporation, Trust and Company*, Manchester, 1950; Albert, *The Turnpike Road System*; R. S. Neale, 'An Equitable Trust in the Building Industry in 1794', *Business History*, 7(2), July 1965; L. E. Davis and D. C. North, *Institutional Change and American Economic Growth*, Cambridge, 1971.

themselves in the course of economic development. There was no need for a new élite, and no new élite in fact, until perhaps the twentieth century. Further, without such revolutionary praxis, which was particularly marked in the late seventeenth and early eighteenth centuries, the phenomenon we know as the Industrial Revolution would have been a non-starter and the question we are probing here would be a non-issue.

5

Capitalism
and the Changing Concept
of Property

C. B. Macpherson

It has long been recognised by social and economic historians that the emergence of capitalism was accompanied by changes in the concept and and institutions of property. Some changes have been so fully discussed in the literature, from Weber, Sombart and Tawney on to, say, Viner, that they need only be recalled here. Other changes have not been so much noticed. This paper begins by drawing attention to three such little noticed changes in the concept of property and showing how they, along with the more recognised ones, were either required by capitalism or were a natural result of it. On this basis I go on to argue that as capitalism matures and comes under new pressures, further changes in the concept and institution of property are required, that one of them is already clearly visible, and that others are possible and even probable, and are needed if property is to be consistent with a democratic society.[1]

Changes in the Concept of Property with the Emergence of Capitalism

The three changes to which I wish to draw attention may be listed as follows. (a) Whereas in pre-capitalist society property was understood to comprise common as well as private property, with the rise of capitalism the idea of common property drops virtually out of sight and property is equated with private property — the right of a natural or artificial person to exclude others from some use or benefit of something. (b) Whereas in pre-capitalist society a man's property had generally been seen as a right to a revenue, with capitalism property comes to be seen as a right in or to material things, or even as the things them-

[1] Apart from the opening few pages, this paper comprises the substance of the essay 'A Political Theory of Property' which was first published in my *Democratic Theory: Essays in Retrieval*, Oxford, Clarendon Press, 1973, and is published here by permission of the Clarendon Press.

selves. (c) There is a change in the rationale or justification of private
property: before capitalism, various ethical and theological grounds had
been offered; with the rise of capitalism, the rationale came to be
mainly that property was a necessary incentive to the labour required
by the society.

I shall discuss these in turn, bringing in where appropriate reference
to some more commonly noticed changes, for example that, under
capitalism, property became a right unconditional on the performance
of any social function, that it became more generally alienable, and that
it lost its earlier broad meaning (one's property including a right in one's
life, liberty, honour, conjugal affection, etc.) and became confined to
one's right in material things and revenues.

Property as private property

Property, nowadays, in the general understanding, at all levels from the
usage of social and political theorists to that of the ordinary newspaper
writer and reader, is usually equated with private property — the right
of an individual (or a corporate entity) to exclude others from some use
or benefit of something. So much is this the case that the very notion of
'common property' is sometimes treated as if it were a contradiction in
terms. 'State property' is of course recognised as an existing fact, but
this is a right of a corporate entity — the state or the government or one
of its agencies — to exclude others, not (as common property is, as we
shall see) an individual right not to be excluded.[2]

At first sight, the identification of property with private property
may seem entailed in the very idea of property, for the idea of property
is undoubtedly the idea of an enforceable claim of a person to some use
or benefit of something. It will not be disputed that the very idea of
property, as something over and above mere momentary physical possession or occupancy, is the idea of an enforceable claim, extending over
time, to the use or benefit of something. Property is a claim which the
individual can count on having enforced in his favour by society or the
state, by custom or convention or law.

But it does not follow from this that an individual's property is
confined to his right to exclude others. An enforceable claim of an
individual to some use or benefit of something equally includes his right
not to be excluded from the use or benefit of something which society

[2] The distinction between private property, state property, and common
property, is set out more fully in my introductory essay to a volume of readings
on *Property*, New York, 1973. I have used some passages, without significant
change, in this essay and in that (and also in this and in the concluding essay in
that volume) whenever that seemed the most economical procedure.

or the state has proclaimed to be for common use. Society or the state may declare that some things — for example, common lands, public parks, city streets, highways — are for common use. The right to use them is then a property of individuals, in that each member of the society[3] has an enforceable claim to use them. It need not be an unlimited claim. The state may, for instance, ration the use of public lands, or it may limit the kinds of uses anyone may make of the streets or of common waters (just as it now limits the uses anyone may make of his private property), but the right to use the common things, however limited, is a right of individuals.

The fact that we need some such term as *common* property, to distinguish such rights from the exclusive individual rights which are private property, may easily lead to our thinking that such common rights are not individual rights, but they are. They are the property of individuals, not of the state. The state indeed creates and enforces the right which each individual has in the things the state declares to be for common use. But so does the state create and enforce the exclusive rights which are private property. In neither case does the fact that the state creates the right make it the property of the state. In both cases what is created is a right of individuals. The state creates the rights, the individuals have the rights. Common property is created by the guarantee to each individual that he will not be excluded from the use or benefit of something; private property is created by the guarantee that an individual[4] can exclude others from the use or benefit of something. Both kinds of property, being guarantees to individual persons, are individual rights. It therefore does not follow from the fact that all property consists in enforceable claims of (natural or artificial) individuals that property is logically confined to private property (the right to exclude others).

The now common notion that it is so confined goes back no further than the seventeenth century, where it can be seen to be the product of the new relations of the emergent capitalist society. It is true that from the beginning of argument about property — an argument as old as political theory itself — the argument was mainly about private property. This is not surprising, since it is only the existence of private property

[3] The society may be as small as a medieval village or as large as a nation-state (or even larger, as when international law recognises, for example, right to use the high seas).

[4] Including the artificial individuals created by the state as corporate bodies, which corporate bodies may include, as they do in the case of state property, the state itself or its agents.

that makes property a contentious moral issue. In any case, the earliest extant theorising about property was done in societies which did have private property, though they were also familiar with common property. So, while the argument was mainly about private property, the theorists did not equate it with 'property'. Aristotle could talk about two systems of property, one where all things were held in common and one where all things were held privately, and about mixed systems where land was common but produce was private and where produce was common but land was private: all these he saw as systems of property.

From then on, whether the debate was about the relative merits of private versus common property, or about how private property could be justified or what limits should be put on it, it was private property that bulked largest in the debate. It was attacked by Plato as incompatible with the good life for the ruling class; defended by Aristotle as essential for the full use of human faculties and as making for a more efficient use of resources; denigrated by earliest Christianity; defended by St Augustine as a punishment and partial remedy for original sin; attacked by some heretical movements in medieval (and Reformation) Europe; justified by St Thomas Aquinas as in accordance with natural law, and by later medieval and Reformation writers by the doctrine of stewardship. In all that early controversy, stretching down through the sixteenth century, what was chiefly in question was an exclusive, though limited or conditional, individual right in land and goods.

But in that early period the theorists, and the law, were not unacquainted with the idea of common property. Common property was, by one writer or another, advocated as an ideal, attributed to the primitive condition of mankind, held to be suited only to man before the fall, and recognised as existing alongside private property in such forms as public parks, temples, markets, streets, and common lands. Indeed Jean Bodin, the first of the great early modern political theorists, in making a strong case at the end of the sixteenth century for modern private property, argued that in any state there must also be some common property, without which there could be no sense of community and hence no viable state: part of his case for private property was that without it there could be no appreciation of common property.

It is only when we enter the modern world of the full capitalist market society, in the seventeenth century, that the idea of common property drops virtually out of sight. So David Hume, who saw the protection of property as the chief business of government, could define property as an individual's right to use to the exclusion of others.[5] That

[5] Cf. Hume's definition, note 9 of this paper.

common property dropped out of sight can be seen as a reflection of the changing facts. From the sixteenth and seventeenth centuries on, more and more of the land and resources in settled countries was becoming private property, and private property was becoming an individual right unlimited in amount, unconditional on the performance of social functions, and freely transferable, as it substantially remains to the present day. Modern private property is indeed subject to certain limits on the uses to which one can put it: the law commonly forbids using one's land or buildings to create a nuisance, using any of one's goods to endanger lives, and so on. But the modern right, in comparison with the feudal right which preceded it, may be called an absolute right in two senses: it is a right to dispose of, or alienate,[6] as well as to use; and it is a right which is not conditional on the owner's performance of any social function.

This of course was exactly the kind of property right needed to let the capitalist market economy operate. If the market was to operate fully and freely, if it was to do the whole job of allocating labour and resources among possible uses, then all labour and resources had to become, or be convertible into, this kind of property. The market had to be allowed to allocate labour and resources not only between the alternative uses that could be said to be determined by the effective demands of consumers, but also (and overridingly) between the alternatives of more for accumulation of capital and more (or more immediate) satisfaction of the demand for consumption goods. As the capitalist

[6] The right to alienate one's property in land, though inconsistent with the feudal principle of personal tenure, was indeed won in the thirteenth century, long before the emergence of modern capitalism: the Statute of *Quia Emptores* (1290) gave that right to tenants in fee simple. But at the same time the landowners were equally interested in the right to tie up their property: they 'did not wish to be deprived of the power of making family settlements, which would be secure, not only against voluntary alienation by their heirs, but also against the involuntary alienation which followed upon a conviction for treason or felony' (Sir William Holdsworth, *Essays in Law and History*, Oxford, 1946, p.105). The right to *prevent* future alienation was established by the statute *De Donis Conditionalibus* in 1285, and was widely exercised, so that thenceforth much of the land was not alienable. In the subsequent centuries various ways around this inalienability were tried, but it was not till the end of the seventeenth century that the courts were able 'to confirm the legality of the expedients devised from circumventing the statute *De Donis*, to pronounce illegal all attempts to create an unbarrable entail, and finally to evolve the rule against perpetuities' (ibid., p.107). To say that alienability is one of the features that distinguishes modern from medieval property is not to say that it was absent from still earlier societies. Alienability was generally recognised in classical Greece and Rome, whose economies were more market-based than those of feudal societies. All market societies require alienability of property in some degree; the full market society requires it in the highest degree.

market economy found its feet and grew, it was expected to, and did, take on most of this work of allocation. As it did so, it was natural that the very concept of property should be reduced to that of *private* property — an exclusive, alienable, 'absolute' individual or corporate right in things.

Property as a right to (or even as) material things, rather than as a right to a revenue

In pre-capitalist England, property had generally been seen as a right to a revenue (whether in the form of services or produce or money) rather than as a right to specific material things, and had not been seen as the material things themselves.[7] This reflected the real situation: until the emergence of the capitalist economy, property had in fact mainly been a right to a revenue rather than a right to a thing. In the first place the great bulk of property was then property in land, and a man's property in a piece of land was generally limited to certain uses of it and was often not freely disposable. Different people might have different rights in the same piece of land, and many of those rights were not fully disposable by the current owner of them either by sale or bequest.[8] The property he had was obviously some right in the land, and usually the right to a revenue from the land, not the land itself. And in the second place, another substantial segment of property consisted of those rights to a revenue which were provided by such things as corporate charters, monopolies granted by the state, tax farming rights, and the incumbency of various political and ecclesiastical offices. Clearly here too the property was the right to a revenue, not a right to any specific material thing.

The change in common usage, to treating property as the things themselves, came with the spread of the capitalist market economy, which brought the replacement of the old limited rights in land by virtually unlimited rights, and the replacement of the old privileged

[7] Medieval English law did treat rights as 'things' (that is did treat present and future and partial rights in material things, chiefly land, as legal 'things'), but it did not treat things (in the modern sense of material things) as property. Somewhat as in Roman law, where *res* included *res corporales* and *res incorporales* ('things' which are not material things), so in English law there were *corporeal* and *incorporeal hereditaments.* These were property, but in each case the property was a right in the material thing, not the material thing itself: a *corporeal hereditament* was 'a *present* right to enjoy the possession of land either personally or through tenants', an *incorporeal hereditament* 'a future right to possession or a right to use for a special purpose land in possession of another, e.g. a right of way' (Topham's *Real Property*, 3rd ed., London, 1921, pp.7-8; cf. C. Reinold Noyes, *The Institution of Property*, New York, 1936, pp.267-8).

[8] See note 6 of this paper.

rights to commercial revenues by more marketable properties in actual capital, however accumulated. As rights in land became more absolute, and parcels of land became more freely marketable commodities, it became natural to think of the land itself as the property. And as aggregations of commercial and industrial capital, operating in increasingly free markets and themselves freely marketable, overtook in bulk the older kinds of movable wealth based on charters and monopolies, the capital itself, whether in money or in the form of actual plant, could easily be thought of as the property. The more freely and pervasively the market operated, the more this was so. It appeared to be the things themselves, the actual parcels of land and portions of commercial capital, not just rights in them, that were exchanged in the market. In fact the difference was not that things rather than rights in things were exchanged, but that previously unsalable or not always salable rights in things were now salable; or, to put it differently, that limited and not always salable right *in* things (land, and trading privileges that were in effect capital) were being replaced by virtually unlimited and salable rights *to* things (land and actual capital).

As property became increasingly salable absolute rights to things, the distinction between the right and the thing was easily blurred, more easily so because, with these changes, the state became more and more an engine for guaranteeing the full right of the individual to the disposal as well as use of things. The state's protection of the right could be so much taken for granted that one did not have to look behind the thing to the right. The thing itself became, in common parlance, the property.

This usage, which is still today the commonplace one, has on the whole been avoided by legal and political writers, who have fairly steadily seen that property is a right not a thing, although it can occasionally be found in theorists as early as the eighteenth century.[9] But

[9] Hume, for instance, although generally quite clearly stating that property is a right in something, or 'such a relation betwixt a person and an object as permits him, but forbids any other, the free use and possession of it, without violating the laws of justice and moral equity' (*Treatise of Human Nature*, Book II, Part II, section X, Green and Grose ed., Vol. II, p.105), did at least once slip into the other usage: 'A man's property is some object related to him' (ibid., Book III, Part II, section II; Vol. II, p.264). Bentham in 1789 noted, disapprovingly, the common usage: 'It is to be observed, that in common speech, in the phrase *the object of a man's property*, the words *the object of* are commonly left out; and by an ellipsis, which, violent as it is, is now become more familiar than the phrase at length, they have made that part of it which consists of the words *a man's property* perform the office of the whole' (*Introduction to the Principles of Morals and Legislation*, chapter 16, section 26, Harrison ed., p.337, n.1). The common usage is now recognised by legal writers (for example J. C. Vaines, *Personal Property*, 3rd ed., London, 1962, p.3), perforce, since the common usage had crept into the courts (cf. Noyes, *The Institution of Property*, pp.356-7).

what the political theorists generally did do, from the seventeenth century on, was to treat property as rights in material things rather than as rights to revenues. The reason for this is presumably the same as the reason for the common misusage: with the rise of the capitalist market economy, the bulk of actual property shifted *from* often non-transferable rights to a revenue from land, monopolies, charters, and offices, *to* transferable rights in freehold land, salable leases, physical plant, and money, which is a claim at will on any of those material things. It is in this sense that the change from property as rights to revenues, to property as rights in material things, can be seen as the product of the rise of capitalist market relations.

Property as the incentive to necessary labour

The idea that the main function of the institution of property is to be an incentive to the labour required by a society is also new in the seventeenth century. Before then, property was held to be needed (and justified) mainly for other reasons, for example to enable men to express their human essence (Aristotle), or to counteract their sinful nature (Augustine). Reasoning from such bases did justify some exclusive individual property, but only for the fully rational (or fully human) individuals, not for slaves or serfs.

What required a new case for exclusive individual property in the seventeenth century, that is, for turning virtually *all* property into *exclusive* private property, was the change in fact and in ideology that came with the rise of capitalist relations. The change in fact was that all men were being brought to the valuation of the market, and were being made free to contract in the market. The change in ideology was that all men were now asserted to be capable of a fully human life (clearly, by the Levellers; grudgingly and ambiguously by Locke). Given the assertion of the natural equal humanity of all men, it became logically necessary to assert a property right open to everyone. But it was impossible to derive, from human needs alone, an exclusive individual right, open to everyone, in land and capital. For it was assumed that land and capital always necessarily would be, as they always had been, held by less than all men, and on that assumption need alone could not confer on everyone an exclusive right.

So, if the new kind of property required by the capitalist market society, that is, property as an exclusive, alienable right to all kinds of material things including land and capital, was to be thought to be justified, the right would have to be based on something more universal than the old feudal or customary class differentials in supposed needs and capacities.

The universal basis was found in 'labour'. Every man had a property in his own labour. And from the postulate that a man's labour was peculiarly, exclusively his own, all that was needed followed. The postulate reinforced the concept of property as exclusion. As his labour was his own, so was that with which he had mixed his labour, and that capital which he had accumulated by means of applying his labour. This was the principle that Locke made central to the liberal concept of property.

The labour justification of individual property was carried down unquestioned in the liberal theory. Even Bentham, scorning natural rights and claiming to have replaced them by utility, rested the property right on labour. Security of enjoyment of the fruits of one's labour was the reason for property: without a property in the fruits and in the means of labour no one would have an incentive to labour, and utility could not be maximised. Mill and Green also held to the labour justification.

> The institution of property when limited to its essential elements, consists in the recognition, in each person, of a right to the exclusive disposal of what he or she have produced by their own exertions, or received either by gift or by fair agreement, without force or fraud, from those who produced it. The foundation of the whole is the right of producers to what they themselves have produced.[10]

> The rationale of property, in short, requires that everyone who will conform to the positive condition of possessing it, viz. labour, and the negative condition, viz. respect for it as possessed by others, should so far as social arrangements can make him so, be a possessor of property himself, and of such property as will at least enable him to develope a sense of responsibility, as distinct from mere property in the immediate necessaries of life.[11]

So the derivation of property in things from the property in one's labour stamped property as an exclusive right from the beginning of the liberal tradition.

It provided a justification of precisely the kind of property that was required by a full capitalist market society. A man's own labour, as well as capital and land, was made so much a private exclusive property as to be alienable, that is, marketable. The concept of property as nothing but an exclusive, alienable, individual right, not only in material things,

[10] J. S. Mill, *Principles of Political Economy*, Book II, chapter 2, section 1.

[11] T. H. Green, *Lectures on the Principles of Political Obligation*, section 221.

but even in one's own productive capacities was thus a creation of capitalist society: it was only needed, and only brought forth, when the formal equality of the market superseded the formal inequality of precapitalist society.

Thus we may say that the now dominant concept of property was, in its three leading characteristics, a creation of the capitalist market society. It was the needs of that society, as of no previous society, that produced first the identification of property with private, exclusive property; second the concept of property as a right to material things rather than a right to a revenue; and third the justification of such property in terms of labour.

Mid-Twentieth-Century Changes in the Concept of Property

The concept of property just outlined, which became dominant with the full development of capitalism in the nineteenth and twentieth centuries, is already undergoing changes. The most general change is that property is again being seen as a right to a revenue or an income, rather than as rights in specific material things. The change is evident in all sectors of advanced capitalist societies: the changed view is common to investors, beneficiaries of the welfare state, independent enterprisers, and wage and salary earners.

Investors, to the extent that they are pure rentiers, have of course always seen their property as a right to a revenue. But with the rise of the modern corporation, and the predominance of corporate property, more individual investors of all sorts become rentiers and become aware that that is what they are. Their property consists less of their ownership of some part of the corporation's physical plant and stock of materials and products than of their right to a revenue from the ability of the corporation to manoeuvre profitably in a very imperfect market. True, an investor may see his property as a right to expected capital gains rather than to expected dividends, but this is still a right to a revenue (a more sophisticated one, less subject perhaps to reduction by the income tax). Moreover, with the spread of affluence and of security-consciousness, increasing numbers of people have some property in the form of rights in pension funds or annuities, if not of rights to a revenue from stocks or bonds. This of course has not turned the whole population into rentiers, but it is making members of all classes more revenue-conscious than many of them were before.

The rise of the welfare state has created new forms of property and distributed them widely — all of them being rights to a revenue. The old-age pensioner, the unemployed, and the unemployable, may have as his sole property the right to such a revenue as his condition entitles him to receive from the state. Where in addition the state provides such things as family allowances and various free or subsidised services, almost everyone has some property in such rights to a revenue.

But while almost everyone may get some of his income from the welfare state, and increasing numbers get some of theirs (at least indirectly) as investors, most people still have to work for most of their income. Their main property is their right to earn an income, whether as self-employed persons or as wage or salary earners. Whichever way they earn their income, they are coming to see their main property as the right to do so, and to see that this depends on factors outside their control.

Those who may still be counted as independent enterprisers — the self-employed, from taxi operators to doctors — find that their property in their enterprises increasingly depends on governmental licences to ply their trade or exercise their profession: their property is an expectation of a revenue dependent on their conformity to increasingly stringent regulations laid down by the state or its agents 'in the public interest'.[12]

However, the bulk of those whose main income is from their work is now made up of wage and salary earners. And they, as we have seen, are increasingly coming to see their property as the right to a job, the right to be employed. Since they are by definition employed by others, that right amounts to a right of access to the means of labour which they do not own. What is new is not the fact, but the increasing perception of it.

That an individual's access to the means of labour is his most important property has been true for most men in most societies. For wherever a society's flow of income requires the current labour of most of its members, and wherever most individuals' incomes depend on their contributing their labour, most men's property in the means of life depends on their access to the means of labour. In a simple society most might have access by communal or tribal rights, or, where there was private property in land but still plenty of land, by owning, that is, having some exclusive right in, the land or materials which were their

---

[12] The proliferation of the regulatory powers of the state, and the extent to which this has replaced the older forms of property by a 'new property' in government licences (and government largesse), is strikingly documented by Professor Charles Reich, 'The New Property', *Yale Law Journal*, 73, April 1964. A shorter version of his paper, with the same title, is printed in *The Public Interest*, no.3, Spring 1966. A substantial part of the longer article is reprinted in my volume on *Property*.

necessary means of labour. In a capitalist society, where most do not own their own means of labour, their right to the means of life is reduced to their right of access to means of labour owned by others.

It was all very well for Locke and subsequent liberal theorists to suggest that a man's labour was his most important property: the fact was that the value of a man's labour was zero if he had no access to land or capital. The value of the property in one's labour depended on one's access to the means of labour owned by others. It has been so ever since the predominance of the capitalist market system. It still is so. One's main property is still, for most men, one's right of access to the means of labour. This, as I have said, is not new.

What is new in the mid-twentieth century is that this fact is being more widely recognised. It was seen in the nineteenth century only by a handful of radicals and socialists: it is now seen by a large part of the non-socialist organised labour movement, which thinks of the worker's main property as his right to the job. This is a considerable transformation of the concept of property. And it can have explosive consequences. For to see as one's property a right to earn an income through employment is to see (or to come close to seeing) as one's property a right of access to some of the existent means of labour, that is, to some of the accumulated productive resources of the whole society (natural resources plus the productive resources created by past labour), no matter by whom they are owned.

An Impending Change in the Concept of Property

It can now be forecast that the concept of property as solely private property, the right to exclude others from some use or benefit of something, which is already a concept of an individual right to a revenue, will have to be broadened to include property as an individual right not to be excluded from the use or benefit of the accumulated productive resources of the whole society.

The forecast is made on two grounds: that property as an exclusive alienable 'absolute' right is no longer as much needed in the quasi-market society of the later twentieth century as it was in the earlier, relatively uncontrolled, full market society; and that democratic pressures on those governments which uphold capitalist property rights are becoming strong enough that any such government which claims also to be furthering a democratic society (that is, to be enabling individuals equally to use and develop their human capacities), will have to acknowledge that property as a right of access must be increasingly an individual right not to be excluded from access.

The change from market to quasi-market society

We noticed above that property as exclusive, alienable, 'absolute', individual, or corporate rights in things was required by the full market society because and insofar as the market was expected to do the whole work of allocation of natural resources and capital and labour among possible uses. In such an autonomous market society there is very little room for common property, since common property by definition withholds from the play of the market those resources in which there is common property and so interferes with total market allocation of resources (and of labour, since the more common property there is, the less dependent on employment, that is, the less compelled to enter his labour in the market, is each individual who lacks material productive resources of his own).

There is of course still a place in capitalist market society for some state property, such as transportation and communications facilities that are necessary for, but not profitable to, private enterprise. But such state property is sharply distinct from common property, as we have seen above. State property may assist, but common property hinders, market allocation.

As long as the market was expected to do the whole job of allocation, then, the concept of property that was needed was the concept of private, exclusive, alienable right. But now, even in the most capitalist countries, the market is no longer expected to do the whole work of allocation. We have moved from market society to quasi-market society. In all capitalist countries, the society as a whole, or the most influential sections of it, operating through the instrumentality of the welfare state and the warfare state — in any case, the regulatory state — is doing more and more of the work of allocation. Property as exclusive, alienable, 'absolute', individual or corporate rights in things therefore becomes less necessary.

This does not mean that this kind of property is any less desired by the corporations and individuals who still have it in any quantity. But it does mean that, as this kind of property becomes less demonstrably necessary to the work of allocation, it becomes harder to defend it as the very essence of property. Again, no one would suggest that the removal or reduction of the necessity of this kind of property would by itself result in the disappearance or weakening of it as the very image of property: positive social pressures would also be required.

Democratic pressures on governments

Democratic pressures for more equitable and more secure access to the means of labour and the means of life are clearly increasing. They are, I think, now reaching such a strength that governments which still uphold the exclusive property rights of a capitalist society, and which claim also, as they all do, that they are promoting a fully democratic society — one in which all individuals are enabled equally to use and develop their human capacities — will have to acknowledge that property can no longer be considered to consist solely of private property — an individual right to exclude others from some use or benefit of something — but must be stretched to cover the opposite kind of individual property, an individual right not to be excluded from the use or benefit of something. This means the creation, by law, either of more common property or of more guaranteed access to the means of labour and the means of life which remain privately owned, that is, a diminution of the extent to which private property, especially in productive resources, is a right to exclude.

The pressure comes from several directions. There is the already mentioned insistence by many sectors of organised labour on 'the right to the job', an insistence which the modern state and its agencies have found themselves in a weak position to resist. There is the markedly increasing public awareness of the menaces of air and water and earth pollution, which are seen as a denial of a human right to a decent environment, a denial directly attributable to the hitherto accepted idea of the sanctity of private (including corporate) property. Air and water, which hitherto had scarcely been regarded as property at all, are now being thought of as common property — a right to clean air and water is coming to be regarded as a property from which nobody should be excluded.

So the identification of property with exclusive private property, which we have seen has no standing in logic, is coming to have less standing in fact. It is no longer as much needed, and no longer as welcomed, as it was in the earlier days of the capitalist market society.

The pressures against it can only be strengthened by the logic of the situation. Private property as an institution has always needed a moral justification. The justification of private property (which became the justification of all property, as capitalism took hold and reduced common property to insignificance) has always ultimately gone back either to the individual right to life at a more than animal level (and hence a right to the means of such a life), or to the right to one's own body, hence to one's own labour, hence to the fruits of one's own labour, and hence also to the means of one's labour.

Sometimes the case is made on a ground that appears to be different from either of these, namely, that individual exclusive property is essential to individual freedom both economic and political — freedom from coerced labour and from arbitrary government. This is the case that Jefferson made much of. He argued convincingly that property in the means of one's own labour was not only rightful in itself but was also an indispensable safeguard of individual liberty. With one's own small property one could not be made subservient. And small property was the great guarantee against government tyranny as well as against economic oppression. It was to secure individual liberty, and all the virtues that can flourish only with sturdy independence, that Jefferson wanted America to remain a country of small proprietors.

This justification of property rests, in the last analysis, on the right to life at a more than animal level: freedom from coerced labour and from arbitrary government are held to be part of what is meant by a fully human life. At the same time this justification is an assertion of the right to the means of labour: the whole point is that by working on his own land or other productive resources a man can be independent and uncoerced. However, while the Jeffersonian argument is a branch of the case resting on the right of life, it is important enough to be treated separately: its emphasis on property as a prerequisite of freedom adds something important to the narrow utilitarian case for property as a prerequisite of a flow of the consumable material means of life. So we have three principles on which individual property is based: the right to the material means of life, the right to a free life, and the right to the (current and accumulated) fruits of one's labour.

It can easily be seen that, in the circumstances of mature capitalism, all three principles require that the concept of property be broadened — that it no longer be confined to the individual right to exclude others, but be extended to include each individual's right not to be excluded from the use or benefit of things, and productive powers, that can be said to have been created by the joint efforts of the whole society. Firstly, a right to the means of life must either be a direct one, irrespective of work, to a share in the society's current output of goods and services, a right not to be excluded from its flow of benefits; or a right to earn an income, which requires that one should not be excluded from the use of the accumulated means of labour. Secondly, a right to the fruits of one's labour requires access to the means of labour, or non-exclusion from the accumulated means of labour. Thirdly, a right to a free life can no longer be secured, as it could in Jefferson's day, by each man having his own small property in his means of labour: it can be secured only by guarantees of access on equal terms to the means of labour that are now mainly corporately or socially owned.

Thus the rationale of property, in any of its three justifications, requires the recognition of property as the right not to be excluded — either the right not to be excluded from a share in the society's whole material output, or the right not to be excluded from access to the accumulated means of labour. Of these, the latter has been up to now much the most important. But this is likely to change.

Beyond Property as Access to the Means of Labour

We can now forecast that the concept of property as essentially access to the means of labour will in turn become inadequate, as and to the extent that technological advances make current human labour less necessary; and that, if property is to be consistent with any real demo-cracy, the concept of property will have to be broadened again to include the right to a share in political power, and, even beyond that, a right to a kind of society or set of power relations which will enable the individual to live a fully human life. This is to take to a higher level the concept of property as the prerequisite of a free life.

Property as political power

The importance to each individual of access to the means of labour will clearly diminish if and insofar as the amount of current human labour required to produce an acceptable flow of the means of life for all diminishes. For as less labour is needed, the requirement to work is less needed. The right to *earn* an income becomes less a prerequisite or corequisite of the right *to* an income.

Already, for technical economic reasons as well as from social and political pressures, the most advanced capitalist countries are beginning to move in the direction of providing a 'guaranteed annual income' or setting up a 'negative income tax'. The effect of such meansures is to give everyone an income (though it may at first be a small one) unrelated to work. If the amount of such income should become substantial, the right to earn an income would clearly decline in importance as a form of property. It is too early to say for certain whether, or when, future increases in the productivity of modern societies will so diminish the amount of socially required human labour that it will become possible to detach entirely income from labour expended. But we can say that, to the extent that this happens, property as a valuable individual right will again change its nature.

The change in that case will be more striking than any of the changes we have seen so far. It will be a change from property as a right of access to the means of labour, to property as a right to the means of a fully human life. This seems to move us back through the centuries, to bring us back again to the idea that property in the means of life (a 'good' life) is the main form of property, as it was for the earliest theorists, for example Aristotle, before emphasis shifted to property in land and capital (the means of producing the means of life).

So it does, but the outcome is not the same. For, in the assumed circumstances of greatly increased productivity, the crucial question will no longer be how to provide a sufficient flow of the material means of life: it will be a question of getting the quality and kinds of things wanted for a full life, and, beyond that, of the quality of life itself. And both of these matters will require a property in the control of the mass of productive resources. If one envisages the extreme of an automated society in which nobody has to labour in order to produce the material means of life, the property in the massed productive resources of the whole society becomes of utmost importance. The property that would then be most important to the individual would no longer be the right of access to the means of labour; it would be instead, the right to a share in the control of the massed productive resources. That right would presumably have to be exercised politically. Political power then becomes the most important kind of property. Property, as an individual right, becomes essentially the individual's share in political power.

This becomes *the* important form of property, not only because it is the individual's guarantee of sharing equitably in the flow of consumables, in some part of which he will of course still need a property in the sense of an exclusive right. It becomes important also because only by sharing the control can he be assured of the means of the good or commodious or free life, which would then be seen to consist of more than a flow of consumables.

Property as a right to a kind of society
If property is to remain justified as instrumental to a full life, it will have to become the right not to be excluded from the means of such a life. Property will, in such circumstances, increasingly have to become a right to a set of social relations, a right to a kind of society. It will have to include not only a right to a share in political power as instrumental in determining the kind of society, but a right to that kind of society which is instrumental to a full and free life.

The idea that individual property extends to, and that a crucially important part of it is, a right to a set of power relations that permits a full life of enjoyment and development of one's human capacities, may seem fanciful. How can such a right be reduced to a set of enforceable claims of the individual (failing which, it would not meet an essential criterion of the idea of property)? It could not easily so be reduced merely by amendments to the existing laws of property. The claims that will have to be made enforceable are much broader than those which 'property' has comprised in the liberal society up to now.

There is, in principle, no reason why such broader claims could not be made enforceable, as certain rights to life and liberty are now. But I am suggesting that the broader claims will not be firmly anchored unless they are seen as property. For, in the liberal ethos which prevails in our liberal-democratic societies, property has more prestige than has almost anything else. And if the new claims are not brought under the head of property, the narrow idea of property will be used, with all the prestige of property, to combat them. In short, the new foreseeable and justifiable demands of the members of at least the most technically advanced societies cannot now be met without a new concept of property.

What makes this urgent is the fact that the conquest of scarcity is now not only foreseeable but actually foreseen. In the conditions of material scarcity that have always prevailed up to now,[13] property has been a matter of a right to a material revenue. With the conquest of scarcity that is now foreseen, property must become rather a right to an immaterial revenue, a revenue of enjoyment of the quality of life. Such a revenue cannot be reckoned in material quantities. The right to such a revenue can be reckoned only as a right to participation in a satisfying set of social relations.

If we achieve this concept of property we shall have reached again, but now on a more effective level, and for more people, that broader idea of property that prevailed in the period just before the individual was at once released and submerged by the capitalist market — the idea that a man has a property not just in the material means of life, but in his life itself, in the realisation of all his active potentialities. It is worth re-emphasising here that in the seventeenth century the word 'property' was used in a far wider sense than it has had ever since then. Political writers in the seventeenth century spoke of a man's property as inclu-

[13] To say that scarcity has always prevailed up to now and that its conquest is now foreseeable is not to say that it has all been the result of hitherto inadequate technology, or that its conquest will be automatically accomplished by technological advances. Much of the scarcity in capitalist societies is created by the very requirements of the system of capitalist production, which generates ever-increasing consumer demands, in relation to which there is scarcity by definition (cf. Essay II, section 4 in my *Democratic Theory: Essays in Retrieval*), and which distributes the whole social output in such a way that the poor are subject to real scarcity. But whether the scarcity is real or artificial, it is scarcity.

ding not only his rights in material things and revenues, but also in his life, his person, his faculties, his liberty, his conjugal affection, his honour, etc.; and material property might be ranked lower than some of the others, as it was specifically by Hobbes.[14]

The fact that property once had such a wider meaning opens up the possibility, which our narrower concept has not allowed, that property may once again be seen as more than rights in material things and revenues. The seventeenth-century broad concept of property may strike us as very odd, even quaint and unrealistic. But it seems odd only because we have become accustomed to a narrow concept which was all that was needed by and suited to a market society in which maximisation of material wealth became the overriding value. Now that we have the possibility, and as I have argued the democratic need, to downgrade material maximisation, the broader concept of property becomes more realistic.

Property can and should become again a right to life and liberty; and it can now, in the measure that we conquer scarcity, become a right to a fuller and freer life, for more people, than was attainable (though it was dreamed of) in the seventeenth century. And the right to live fully cannot be less than the right to share in the determination of the power relations that prevail in the society. Property then, we may say, needs to become a right to participate in a system of power relations which will enable the individual to live a fully human life.

It may *need* to become so, but *can* it become so? My argument has been that both the concept and the actual institution of property need to be broadened in this way if they are to be consistent with the needs and the possibility of a society fully democratic and fully free. I have indicated ways in which the concept, and even the institution, are beginning to change in that direction. Whether or how far those changes will proceed depends on both the degree of democratic pressure on governments and the extent of consciousness of what the issues are, and each of these depends partly on the other. The seriousness of the

---

[14] 'Of things held in propriety, those that are dearest to a man are his own life, & limbs; and in the next degree, (in most men,) those that concern conjugall affection; and after them riches and means of living' (*Leviathan*, chapter 30, pp.382-3, Pelican ed.). Locke, when he defined property in the broad sense, also put life and liberty ahead of 'estate', and 'person' ahead of 'goods' (*Second Treatise of Government*, section 87, 123, 173). On seventeenth-century usage generally, see my *Political Theory of Possessive Individualism*, index entry 'Property'.

obstacles should not be underestimated.[15] Neither, however, should the possibility of their being overcome: not by goodwill, nor by any improbable conversion of ruling élites to a new morality; nor necessarily by traumatic revolutionary action; but by a conjuncture of partial breakdowns of the political order and partial breakthroughs of public consciousness.

The former, it may now be seen, may well come through failures of the system to respond adequately to growing demands for access to the means of labour, that is by failure to put such new limitations on exclusive property rights as are needed to meet those demands. The latter might come naturally enough as a growing, even a fairly sudden, realisation that a new property in the quality of life and liberty is now within reach. And each of these changes would reinforce the other.

---

[15] I have referred to some of the operational difficulties in other essays in my *Democratic Theory: Essays in Retrieval*, for example in the concluding pages of Essays II and III; and have discussed related logical problems in Essays III and V.

6

Beyond Bourgeois Individualism: the Contemporary Crisis in Law and Legal Ideology

Eugene Kamenka and Alice Erh-Soon Tay

middle class, etc., etc., but they have done so, we shall be arguing, with only a partial appreciation of the problem and of the trend of events. For the crisis of law and legal ideology is not merely part of the revitalisation of socialist hostility to the entrepreneurial society or to its successor, the world of multi-national corporations. It is a crisis deeply rooted in nineteenth- and twentieth-century developments: in the course and social ramifications of scientific and technological progress, in the changing conditions of economic production and use, in the vastly increased scale and power of enterprises, in the consequent ever more obvious social interdependence of individuals and units and the growing power of the state and its agencies. The extent to which radical socialists have not fully grasped the point can be seen from the fact that the crisis is not at all confined to the west or to free enterprise societies. It is also to be found in the communist world. There it manifests itself as a crisis within Marxist legal ideology and within the socialist conception of the goal — the spontaneously co-operative, egalitarian, truly human society. The early Marxist-Leninist vision of ultimate communism, in which the administration of men is replaced by the administration of things, in which coercive external norms give way to the settled operation of an internalised consciousness of social and ethical justice, has disintegrated. The crisis in that vision has been dramatised by the bitter struggle between the bureaucratic-administrative realism now espoused by Soviet theorists of law and public administration, and the Maoism of the period of the Great Proletarian Cultural Revolution, with its emphasis on popular participation, the 'mass line' and great leaps forward, on continuous or recurrent social upheavals under the slogan 'Smash All Permanent Rules, Go One Thousand Li A Day'. The struggle is, in fact, a struggle between two central but contradictory elements in Marxism — technological rationality and peasant anarchism.

In the communist world, the tension is between revolutionary transformation and the desire for social stability, between mass campaigns and the provision of social and psychological security for individuals, social spheres and activities, between utopian spontaneity and technical-administrative realism. In the west, the crisis is a crisis in the individualistic view of society, in a legal model attuned to the needs of the individual house- or property-holder, the entrepreneur, the settled citizen living on terms of equality with those around him, secure and confident as an individual in his bearing vis-à-vis the state and the rest of society. Against this, the new demands elevate the interests or 'requirements' of the comparatively poor and/or underprivileged as contrasted with those who are 'at home' with law; they pit the interests of 'society' or of 'humanity' against 'excessive' respect for abstract individual rights and powers, especially proprietorial rights and powers; they tend to see men as social products and not as free moral agents, as people to be cured or helped rather than judged. They are suspicious of lawyers as a profession — in the common law world because they see them as a privileged caste with guild traditions and powers, in continental Europe because they see them as characterless servants of the state. Associated with this, and in spite of a growing hostility to the state and its bureaucratic apparatus, we find an increasing demand that law integrate itself with the general social machinery for achieving the common good. Law in the western world — both at the level of the judicial process and at the level of legislation — is asked to overcome its abstraction and its underlying individualism, to take into account extra-legal powers and social inequalities, to investigate total social situations, to make orders that will require new powers and new attitudes on the part of courts, to cease treating the 'public interest' as an unruly horse or, at best, as just another private interest to be weighed against the rights of individuals, to recognise instead a moral hierarchy of interests, to turn its attention from the past actions, immediate interests and abstract rights of the parties before the court to the social context, the social implications and the future consequences of such actions as a general class. Law is being asked to shift its attention from adjudicating between 'private' interests after they are already in conflict to securing and regulating the conduct of social affairs in the name of the social good.

Despite the extent to which these demands carry with them assumptions and criticisms of a clearly socialist colour, they do not come exclusively or even predominantly from consciously socialist groups. The elevation of the direct appeal to public opinion, the weakening of the conceptions of *intra* and *ultra vires*, the rejection of the traditional notion that social institutions have properly limited functions, and a rather new attitude to property and its social role and responsibility, are part of a general social trend. The Charity Commissioners for England . and Wales noted as early as 1969 the way in which such new tendencies were disturbing established concepts of law in their area:

> One contemporary development which has given us some concern has been the increasing desire of voluntary organisations for 'involvement' in the causes with which their work is connected. Many organisations now feel that it is not sufficient simply to alleviate distress arising from particular social conditions or even to go further and collect and disseminate information about the problems they encounter. They feel compelled also to draw attention as forcibly as possible to the needs which they think are not being met, to rouse

the conscience of the public to demand action and to press for
effective official provision to be made to meet those needs. As a result
'pressure groups', 'action groups' or 'lobbies' come into being. But
when a voluntary organisation which is a charity seeks to develop
such activities it nearly always runs into difficulties through going
beyond its declared purposes and powers. No charity should, of
course, undertake any activity unless it is reasonably directed to
achieving its purposes and is within the powers conferred by the
charity's governing instrument.[1]

This wider concern with activating or placating public opinion, as
distinct from safeguarding or exercising one's specific legal rights and
powers, is now to be met with in all areas. Corporations act in alleged
exercise of their responsibilities not just to their workers or customers,
but to the neighbourhood or the community at large[2] while, in moments
of crisis or upheaval, increasing emphasis is placed on avoiding confrontation, preventing the sharpening of issues, looking to the vague and *ad
hoc* compromise, the agreement to live together, rather than the
determination of strictly legal rights and powers, of legality versus
illegality. Thus, in the aftermath of the events in Columbia University
in May 1968, counsel for the university appeared in court to seek leave

[1] Cited in L. A. Sheridan, 'Charity versus Politics', *Anglo-American Law
Review*, 47, 1973, from the Report of the Commissioners, p.5, para.8.

[2] One has only to examine the annual reports of almost any major American
corporation over the last three years to discover attempts to show that the corporation involved, apart from making profits and often at the expense of that
activity, is exercising 'social responsibility', making a contribution to cleaning the
air and water, providing jobs for minorities, injecting money and talent into
urban studies and projects, and helping generally 'to enhance the quality of life
for everyone' – a development noted and welcomed in the leading article in the
Wall Street Journal of 21 October 1971 and made the subject of a good deal of
pious but confused praise of the new social responsibility of modern American
capitalism, not only by board chairmen and presidents, but by theologians,
economic historians and political scientists. The attempt to claim that business is
service – that private vices are public benefits – is not new; what is new and what
is germane to our topic is the belief that business owes a duty to society, to the
public at large, to underprivileged groups or minorities, and that it must meet
such claims upon it in ways other than by simply doing good, honest business.
This view – the exact opposite of J. P. Morgan's famous 'I owe the public nothing'
– is at sharp variance with the traditional legal conception of the role and duty of
trustees, company directors and other persons exercising power and discretion on
behalf of owners of property. In the United States it is already giving rise to a
body of legal claims or suits, and a body of legal literature, that would have been
unthinkable twenty years ago. It is something of an extension of the principle in
Donoghue v. Stevenson to file suit to compel a corporation to disclose whether
there are harmful additives in the foodstuffs it markets, but to file suit to compel
that corporation to hire more blacks in the name of social justice is to step right
outside the realm of private law.

132

to withdraw an application for an injunction to restrain the student trespassers. A university, he said, was like a big family and in a family justice was best done privately.

Behind this shift in social and ideological attitudes is a curious mixture of extreme personal individualism — the cult of the individual personality as an emotional rather than as a political or legal unit[3] — and a collectivism or étatism in which the state is no longer seen so much as the centre of society, as the carrier of moral values, but as rather the limitless provider of the pre-conditions of the good life. The individualism, the elevation of emotional security, of personal dignity, of the right to do one's own thing, is no doubt directly related to relative affluence and a prolonged period of education devoted to nurturing the conception that self-expression is the ultimate goal of life and the birthright of modern man. It underlies what is confusedly expressed by the more strident as a demand for 'participation' — often more a demand for social, industrial and legal recognition of the importance of the individual *as a person*, of his *feelings* and his *integrity*, than a demand for lasting and structured arrangements for genuinely popular control.[4] It is the real content of the objection to the abstraction and alienation that is seen as inherent in traditional legal structures and ways of proceedings, which is taken to subordinate the living individual to abstract impersonal rules, to what appears as the independent power of words and the requirements of processes and interests divorced from their alleged human content or function.[5]

Together with all this, however, and as a crucial part of it, is the appreciation, the taking for granted indeed, of the limitless power, wealth and capacity of the state and of major social and capitalist institutions. The scale of property has become so vast, the sources from

[3] A cult that accounts for the enormous revival of interest in Feuerbach, and a tendency to read even Marx — let alone Jesus — through Feuerbachian spectacles.

[4] To say this is not to decry the movement for participation as such. The demand for 'human' conditions of work and 'human' social relations in the direction and administration of labour grows naturally with the increase in human productivity, affluence, education and professional skill. It is being strengthened, in a very significant way, by the increasing scale of both trade unions and enterprises at the very time when the individual worker is subjected to the effects and disturbances of rapid technological innovations — effects and disturbances often first felt by the men on the shop floor and not at all easily predicted in advance or even taken account of when they do occur by centralised and therefore remote union secretariats or employer-managements.

[5] For the remarkably modern statement of this position vis-à-vis law in Ludwig Feuerbach's ethical fragments see Eugene Kamenka, *The Philosophy of Ludwig Feuerbach*, London and New York, 1970, p.136.

which it draws its wealth so multifarious and pervasive, and its soci[
effects and ramifications so great, that modern man is having increasing
difficulty in thinking of property as private, as the concretisation of an
individual will reifying itself in land or objects, as a walled-in area into
which others may not enter. There is, in other words, a shift of attention
from the property whose paradigm is the household, the walled-in or
marked-off piece of land, the specific bales that make up a cargo or
consignment, to the corporation, the hospital, the defence establishment,
the transport or power utility whose 'property' spreads throughout the
society and whose existence is dependent upon subsidies, state protection, public provision of facilities, etc. In these circumstances, a view of
society and a view of property as a collection of isolated and isolable
windowless monads that come into collision only externally and as a
departure from the norm becomes untenable. Property becomes social
in the sense that its base and its effects can no longer be contained
within the framework of the traditional picture. The major sphere of
social life passes from the private to the public, not merely in the sense
that more and more activity is state activity, but in the sense that more
and more 'private' activity becomes public in its scale and its effect, in
the sense that the oil company is felt to be as 'public' as the state elec-
tricity utility, the private hospital and the private school, with their
growing need for massive state subsidies, as public as the municipal hospital and the state school. This explains one of the most striking of
modern phenomena – the decline in respect for private property, the
popularity of the sit-in, of the demand for *access* as independent of
ownership and as something that ought to be maintainable against it.

Society, then, we are arguing, is being revolutionised just as and
largely because technology is being revolutionised. There are no longer
boundaries that one can draw around one's self and one's possession. It
is the much more urgent sense of social interconnection, of the destruction of social and individual boundaries, which accounts for the declining
confidence among political ideologists in gradual and limited social and
legal reform, in Karl Popper's concept of piecemeal social engineering.

Among lawyers, the predilection for radical and sweeping reform, for
wholesale transformation of the law, is no doubt very much less marked.
Nevertheless, the Law Commissions in England and those reforming
and revising the laws in other countries are going, under the pressure of
social demands, very far beyond the mere tidying-up and rationalisation
of existing law, and even beyond cautious piecemeal social engineering.
It is not only that more and more private areas become public areas and
that more and more private law becomes public law. It is also that the

whole range of legal reforms is fundamentally undermining what many have seen as the specifically legal tradition in society — the tradition connected with a conception of the distinction between law and morality, between law and administration and between law and politics, with the doctrine of the separation of powers, with the concepts of justiciability, competence and jurisdiction and the admittedly defeasible presumption in favour of the rights of the citizen against those of the state and the rest of society.

The shift in matrimonial law from the concept of the matrimonial offence to the concept of the irretrievable breakdown of marriage will be welcomed by many — as it is, on the whole, by us — but its consequences for the nature of that branch of law and the role of the administering tribunals (they will hardly be courts any more) will be very great indeed. Tort, so strongly permeated by the spirit of private law, has long been losing its social and legal pre-eminence. In its traditional form, it is becoming a law suited only to the resolution of minor matters of day-to-day living. Labour or industrial law — the recognition that work in modern society can no longer be dealt with as nothing more than a particular kind of contract that the worker enters 'freely' — is not, whatever it may be, a part of private law. It is, indeed, like the concept of the law of any area — whether it be the law of broadcasting, or fishery, or of the environment — the dissolution of private law, the recognition that these areas cannot be subsumed under the categories of a coherent and developed system of private law, with its emphasis on individual rights and duties, concepts of fault, and *mens rea*, and its sharp limiting of the matters before the court.

The conception of law threatened, undermined or frontally attacked by the demands and developments outlined above is the conception central to the classical liberal individualist ideal of political democracy and the rule of law as ideologised in the American Declaration of Independence, the United States Constitution and the Declaration of the Rights of Man and of the Citizen proclaimed as part of the French Revolution. The critics of this conception of law perceive, whether consciously or unconsciously, that law is not merely a passive tool, a set of decrees wielded like isolatable thunderbolts to protect the interests and authority of a ruler or ruling class. They instinctively recognise that a system of law, with its concepts, principles and procedures, carries with it and rests upon a social and political philosophy, an implicit view of man and his relation to society. They claim, explicitly or implicitly, that the legal ideology associated with liberal democracy is not a timeless phenomenon, a deduction from the word or concept 'law' which sits enthroned in heaven, ministered to by its angels — *the* juristic concepts. It is rather the product and the foundation of a specific view of law and social organisation and of a specific type of society; it shapes man far more than it is shaped by him or by his allegedly 'essential' requirements. The Marxist-socialist account of the matter might appear to be relatively simple: just as capitalist law came to replace feudal law, so socialist law is now coming to replace capitalist law — the elevation of the social interest is replacing the individualistic structure of private rights and duties. The difficulty, however, lies in the very concept of socialist law, a concept over which Marxists have fought bitterly and of which socialists generally have never given a coherent account. It is not enough, nor of course is it especially plausible, to say that feudal law is the expression of the interest of the feudal landlord, capitalist law the expression of the interest of the bourgeoisie, and socialist law the expression of the interest of the proletariat or, ultimately, of the people as a whole. The crisis we are discussing is a crisis in the *form* of law, the result of its inability, on its existing form and principles, to accommodate the new content and role being demanded of it. Socialism itself, both in the east and the west, is ambivalent and uncertain about its conception of the proper form of law and its precise relation to the forms developed under capitalism and the rule of private law. Lip service, no doubt, is still paid to the notion that the ultimate victory of socialism-communism means the withering away of law, but no one seriously believes any longer that it will be replaced by the popular opinions and popular actions of an unstructured community, discussing its problems in what used to be the market-place. To grasp the problem and to come toward a solution, one needs a distinction more subtle, less specifically evolutionary and less Austinian in its attitude to law than the Marxist attempt to distinguish types of law in terms of the ruling class whose interest the law is supposed to serve. We need a distinction that takes into account and explains quite fundamental differences in the form of law, in the view of man and society that underlies it and gives it shape. Elsewhere, drawing on the work of Ferdinand Tönnies and Max Weber, and attempting to incorporate the insights of two great Marxist theorists of law, Karl Renner and E. B. Pashukanis, we have attempted to show that the problem can be solved by recognising the existence of three competing legal-administrative traditions that may and do co-exist within any one society and any one body of law, but which pull in different directions and which display themselves at different periods and in different places in varying strengths. These types, we have argued, are the *Gemeinschaft* type, the *Gesellschaft* type and the bureaucratic-administrative type.[6] Each of these, as we see it, has a structure of its own, in which substantive law, procedure and underlying, implicit legal and social philosophy are closely intertwined and strive toward a certain systematic coherence, carrying with them a view of man, of society and of the nature and tasks of social administration or regulation.

In the *Gemeinschaft* type of social regulation, punishment and resolution of disputes, the emphasis is on law and regulation as expressing the will, the internalised norms and traditions of an organic community, to whom each individual member is part of the social family. Here there tends to be no sharp distinction, if there is any formal distinction at all, between the private and the public, between the civil wrong and the criminal offence, between politics, justice and administration, between political issues, legal issues and moral issues. There is little emphasis on the abstract, formal criteria of justice and the person at the bar of judgment is there, in principle, as a whole man, bringing with him his status, his occupation and his environment, all of his history and his social relations. He is not there as an abstract right-and-duty-bearing individual, as just a party to the contract or as the ower of a specific and limited duty to another. Justice is thus substantive, directed to a particular case in a particular social context and not to the establishing of a general rule or precedent except, as we shall see, where the taboos protecting the social structure are involved. The formalism of procedure in this type of justice can be considerable, but they are linked with magical taboo notions, they are emotive in content and concrete in formulation; they are not based on abstract rationalistic conceptions of justice and procedure. They are not frankly and openly utilitarian, directed toward the rational pursuit of individual goals and individual convenience. Consider only the ritualistic character of *sala* and *gewerida*, the notion of culpability in the *deodand* and the consequent demand for its surrender, the quasi-magical overtones of the insistence on strict liability, the central role played by the *kowtow* in traditional Chinese concepts of judicial procedure and the similarly central role ascribed to the spiritual *kowtow*, the culprit's recognition of guilt and desire to repent and reform, in both Christian and communist judicial procedure. For the *Gemeinschaft* is above all, as Tönnies noted, a religious society held together by a common religious ideology that cannot tolerate the breaker of its taboos; its symbols are the seal and the pillory. The historical key to the *Gemeinschaft*, as both Tönnies and Renner

[6]See Eugene Kamenka and Alice Erh-Soon Tay, 'Beyond the French Revolution: Communist Socialism and the Concept of Law', *University of Toronto Law Journal*, 21, 1971, pp.109-40.

recognised, is the agrarian *household* which is not a simple, undifferentiated item of property but a complex economic, social and political unit, in which the religious, the familial, the educational, the political, the legal, the administrative and the charitable are all held together, in which property is the locus of both economic and civic power and responsibility. In it, the private and the public are indistinguishable.

The *Gesellschaft* type of law and legal regulation is in all respects the very opposite of the *Gemeinschaft* type. It arises out of the growth of individualism and of the protest against the status society and the fixed locality; it is linked with social and geographical mobility, with cities, commerce and the rise of the bourgeoisie. It assumes a society made up of atomic individuals and private interests, each in principle equivalent to the other, capable of agreeing on common means while maintaining their diverse ends. It emphasises formal procedure, impartiality, adjudicative justice, precise legal provisions and definitions and the rationality and predictability of legal administration. It is oriented to the precise definition of the rights and duties of the individual through a sharpening of the point at issue and not to the day-to-day *ad hoc* maintenance of social harmony, community traditions and organic solidarity; it reduces the public interest to another, only *sometimes* overriding, private interest. It distinguishes sharply between law and administration, between the public and the private, the legal and the moral, between the civil obligation and the criminal offence. Its model for all law is contract and the *quid pro quo* associated with commercial exchange, which also demands rationality and predictability. It has difficulty in dealing with the state or state instrumentalities, with corporations, social interests and the administrative requirements of social planning or of a process of production unless it reduces them to the interests of a 'party' to the proceedings confronting another 'party' on the basis of formal equivalence and legal interchangeability. Its conception of contract as the basis of social life developed, at least partly, in connection with the power to contract for and to control labour that is separated from the household and thus reduced to the abstract status of the factory hand, whose life outside the factory is irrelevant to the contract. Property in the *Gesellschaft* is the power to control and to dispose of according to one's will to an extent undreamt of in the *Gemeinschaft*: waste, improvement, wardships, easements lose their social importance, everything in principle becomes saleable, alienable, exchangeable. The economic is divorced from the social, the political, the religious, and treated in its own abstract terms. To the maxim *Nulle terre sans seigneur*, *Gesellschaft* law counterposes the maxim *L'argent n'a pas de maître*. For all its relative modernity and sophistication, however, the *Gesellschaft*, legally and ideologically, is above all a simplifying phenomenon, an attempt to reduce all things to the same level and to the same currency, the single medium of exchange. It is the *Gemeinschaft* which is legally, politically, socially, culturally complex.

Gemeinschaft-type law takes for its fundamental pre-supposition and concern the organic community. *Gesellschaft*-type law takes for its fundamental pre-supposition and concern the atomic individual, theoretically free and self-determined, limited only by the rights of other *individuals*. These two 'ideal types' of law necessarily stand in opposition to each other, though in actual legal systems at any particular time both strains will be present and each will have to make accommodations to the other. In the bureaucratic-administrative type of regulation, the pre-supposition and concern is neither an organic human community nor an atomic individual; the pre-supposition and concern is a non-human abstracted ruling interest, public policy or on-going activity, of which human beings and individuals are subordinates, functionaries or carriers. The *Gesellschaft*-type law concerning railways is oriented toward the rights of people whose interests may be harmed by the operation of railways or people whose activities may harm the rights of the owners or operators of railways seen as individuals exercising individual rights. Bureaucratic-administrative regulations concerning railways take for their object the efficient running of railways or the efficient execution of tasks and attainment of goals and norms (the transportation of 'the people') which are set by the authorities, or the 'community', or the bureaucracy as its representative. Individuals as individuals are the *object* of some of these regulations but not their *subject*; the subject, at most, is 'the community'. Individuals are relevant not as persons having rights and duties vis-à-vis the transport system as individuals, but as consumers or functionaries, as part of the railway-running process and its organisation, as people receiving benefits as consumers and having duties and responsibilities as functionaries. Such people are seen as carrying out roles, as not standing in a 'horizontal' relation of equivalence to the railway organisation or to all their fellow workers, but as standing in defined 'vertical' relations of subordination and sub-subordination. For this reason, bureaucratic-administrative legislation typically envisages and provides for subordinate legislation and regulation as an integral part of its legislation *for an area of activity or social life. Gesellschaft* law, characteristically, makes no such provision; it regards its rules as the general, pervasive and essentially exhaustive rules of conduct for all relations between individuals, which are to be applied to any circumstances at all, though no doubt in the light of particular conditions and experience that may be recognised and systematised in a body of precedents. Subordinate legislation for *Gesellschaft* law is not truly subordinate at all; it is local as opposed to national, administrative or regulatory rather than truly legal — concerned typically with the duty to stay on pathways, to purchase a dog licence, to submit to inspection of one's premises.

In developed industrial societies, as law begins to move to the control of finance and credit, as the large public corporation replaces the individual mill owner-manager as the paradigm of the capitalist propertyholder, the conception of property loses its individual basis and the emphasis shifts from external relations between individual propertyowners to internal direction and control. This is what Karl Marx foresaw as the socialisation of capital from within; it involves the elevation of administration over ownership and a new bureaucratic-administrative concept of property, the Soviet concept of operational management. In the west, too, bureaucratic-administrative requirements — the licensing of innkeepers, pharmacists, etc. — produced the need for a similar concept: the licensee, the person nominated under the licence, who is something more than the nominal defendant required by *Gesellschaft* law, who has duties of overseeing as well as those of being legally liable.[7] At the same time, the growing concern with and interest in the law of certain areas — broadcasting, fishery, trade practices, the environment — is necessarily one that requires bureaucratic-administrative forms and attitudes: it seeks to regulate an activity and not to adjudicate in collisions between individuals; its fundamental concern is with consequences rather than with fault or *mens rea*, with public need or public interest, or the interest of the activity itself, rather than private rights and individual duties. Bureaucratic-administrative regulation, as Pashukanis saw, elevates the socio-technical norm against the private right of the *Gesellschaft* and the traditions and organic living together of the *Gemeinschaft*.

Bureaucratic-administrative regulation, thus, is quite distinct from both *Gemeinschaft* and *Gesellschaft* law, but it does not stand in quite

[7]Comparatively recent attempts, such as that of D. R. Harris, in A. G. Guest (ed.), *Oxford Essays in Jurisprudence*, London, 1961, pp.69-106, to deny that there is a unitary concept of possession in the common law gain their force from something they do not take account of — not from the fact that there is a special concept of possession in the criminal law or that courts are thoroughly utilitarian and unsystematic, but from the fact that the traditional concept of possession does not lend itself well to situations in which operational management is the key factor. Licensing laws have long recognised this by requiring a nominee, that is, by recognising the possible divorce between ownership (or possession even) and management.

the sharp uncompromising opposition to them that they do to each other; pursuing different aims, it nevertheless finds points of contact and affinity with each of the other forms. The bureaucratic-administrative emphasis on an interest to which individuals are subordinate, on the requirements of a total concern or activity, brings it to the same critical rejection of *Gesellschaft* individualism as that which is characteristic of the *Gemeinschaft*; it gives it a similar interest in maintaining harmonious functioning, in allowing scope for *ad hoc* judgment and flexibility, in assessing a total situation and the total effects of its judgment in that situation. At the same time, bureaucratic-administrative regulation is a phenomenon of large-scale, non-face-to-face administration, in which authority has to be delegated. As the scale grows, bureaucratic rationality — regularity and predictability, the precise definition of duties and responsibilities, the avoidance of areas of conflict and uncertainty — becomes increasingly important. This requirement of bureaucratic-rationality in the bureaucratic-administrative system stands in tension with *Gemeinschaft* attitudes, unless they are strictly limited in scope. It finds a certain common ground with the distinguishing features of *Gesellschaft* law in the emphasis on the universality of rules and the precise definition of terms, in the important role ascribed to the concepts of *intra* and *ultra vires*, in the rejection of arbitrariness and of the excessive use of *ad hoc* decisions to the point where they threaten this rationality. This is why it is possible to do what many common lawyers are so prone to do — to use private law forms for public law purposes. But it is possible to do so only to a limited extent — both the spirit and the content sooner or later burst through to destroy the form.

The contemporary crisis of law and legal ideology, in our view, then, is a crisis of *Gesellschaft* law, a crisis in its capacity to deal with what are seen as the urgent problems of our time and, consequently, in its claim to legitimacy. *Gesellschaft* law works best where the fiction of legal equality and interchangeability is accompanied by a reasonable approximation to social equality and interchangeability, where parties do confront each other as relatively independent, 'free', and equal actors. It is seriously threatened by major and relevant inequalities of power, education or social position which undermine the *Gesellschaft* conception of legal capacity as well as of the equality of the parties. It is not attuned, in its underlying individualism, to the fact of social interconnection and interdependence or to the supraindividual requirements of social activities and social living. As these achieve greater and greater independent power, confront the individual as something beyond his control, requiring massive social organisation and/or state intervention,

Gesellschaft law is further undermined. This, fundamentally, is the crisis we are facing today, of which the radical critique of capitalism, the talk of alienation and propaganda and sentiments of a socialist colour generally are symptoms rather than causes.

Socialists themselves have not diagnosed the disease fully and have certainly not provided a remedy because of their fundamental ambivalence in relation to *Gesellschaft* law. Socialism was the critique of the ideology of the French Revolution, the ideology of the *Gesellschaft* with its emphasis on legal and political liberty, equality, fraternity, seen in individualistic terms, in the light of the realities of the Industrial Revolution, which readily increased social inequalities, which extended enormously the social ramifications of property. But socialists vacillated, as they still vacillate today, between a backward-looking elevation of the *Gemeinschaft*, purportedly shorn of its emphasis on tradition and hierarchy, and the Saint-Simonian étatist insistence on rational social planning through state and centralised agencies. The socialist critique of *Gesellschaft* law, in other words, conflates *Gemeinschaft* values and bureaucratic-administrative values. The history of socialism is the history of shifts and conflicts between these two ideologies, each necessary to the complete socialist critique of capitalist society, to socialism's claim to be at once the negation of capitalism and the consummation of modern industrial and post-industrial society.

The typology suggested here does not imply a simple, straightforward evolutionary schema, in which each stage is replaced by its successor and then thrown into the dustbin of history. It recognises, on the contrary, that *Gemeinschaft*, *Gesellschaft* and bureaucratic-administrative strains will co-exist in all, or at least in most, societies, standing in comparatively complex relation with each other. We are thus able to recognise the important *Gesellschaft* element in European feudalism, its emphasis on contract, its conception of charters and privileges maintainable against the giver, as opposed to the strong bureaucratic-administrative strain in the laws of Imperial China, despite the predominant *Gemeinschaft* character of each of these societies.

We are also able to recognise the existence of *Gesellschaft* strains, even of strong *Gesellschaft* strains, in the law of early heavily commercial societies, Rome and Babylon. Social relations, even in allegedly 'primitive' societies, are complex and they will display at least incipient *Gemeinschaft*, *Gesellschaft* and bureaucratic-administrative characteristics at all stages of social development. But certain historical periods and certain countries do provide us with classical epochs in which a particular strain comes out with special clarity, comes to self-consciousness as it were, serves as a paradigm that illuminates in a new way our understanding of the present, of the past, and of the foreseeable future. Nineteenth-century bourgeois commercial society gave us such a paradigm for the *Gesellschaft*, a paradigm that has become even better understood as *Gesellschaft* conceptions come under fire from *Gemeinschaft* and bureaucratic-administrative quarters in both the nineteenth and the twentieth centuries. But complexity does not disappear — the reduction of all social relations to the cash nexus which Marx, at one stage, postulated as the inescapable trend of capitalism, has never been fully consummated. Our modern *Gesellschaft* has been made bearable because it was able to contain innumerable *Gemeinschaften*, from the family to the university to the political party. It is one of the paradoxes of the student revolution, of the movement for women's liberation, and of much radical criticism generally, that it is most effective against the remaining *Gemeinschaft* structures in our society, that it seeks to turn them into *Gesellschaften* with clearly defined constitutions and rights, even while the talk is of community and social togetherness. Nevertheless, in the western world there is no doubt that the immediate trend is toward the immeasurable strengthening and extension of bureaucratic-administrative strains at the expense of *Gesellschaft* and *Gemeinschaft* strains, even though *Gemeinschaft* ideology, the emphasis on not treating men as objects, will provide a certain humanising cosmetic for bureaucratic practice, will impose on it a certain style. Courts will increasingly become tribunals; punishment may become 'cure'; damages will be replaced by insurance. But in our own society, *Gesellschaft* traditions are still strong; they will continue to colour, and to mitigate the great dangers to liberty and human dignity involved in both *Gemeinschaft* and bureaucratic-administrative conceptions.

In the East, in communist countries, similar strains and tensions have been at work. The conflict between them has been skilfully used by the Soviet regime in particular to contain each one. The *Gemeinschaft* strain, linked with the anarchist component in Marxism and drawing to some extent on the traditions of the peasant *mir*, rejects legalistic and bureaucratic methods of control and relies on spontaneous, informal community pressure, 'revolutionary justice', and social opinion. It puts a heavy premium on conformity, in principle rejects completely legal safeguards that would protect the individual from social persecution (consider the trial of Brodsky before the Leningrad Comrades' Court) and provides, in Soviet conditions, forms of social pressure that are hard to resist and are yet almost completely manipulable by the party and the authorities.

The second strain, the administrative-bureaucratic strain, sees law as concerned with social regulation in terms of state and party interests and/or developmental policies. It is still the strongest strain in the Soviet Union; it is entrenched in various ways in the Civil and Criminal Codes, which see all rights as *granted by the state* and as wrongs those activities which are *socially* dangerous. It accounts for the concern, in Soviet administration and Soviet legal proceedings, with bureaucratic correctness and pedantry rather than the *Gesellschaft* concern with an adjudicative conception of 'natural justice' and for the frankly inquisitorial role of the court, linking it with the bureaucratic-administrative traditions of French law.

The third strain, the *Gesellschaft* strain, stems from the emphasis on socialist legality, impartial arbitration and formal constitutional guarantees beginning with the new economic policy and given some ideological foundation, if very little practical application, during the period of Stalin. It involves at least lip service to constitutionality, independence of the judiciary, formal legal correctness and the protection, even if in a limited way, of some individual rights and some civil liberties. The de-Stalinisation campaign initiated by Krushchev raised the expection that this strain in Soviet life would be strengthened; in the area of civil liberties it has in fact since been weakened. Nevertheless, the concern with a certain stability, with an attempt to assure citizens and enterprises of a formal framework within which social and economic life can be expected to move, came out in the defeat in 1959 and 1960 of proposals for a Code of Economic Law, on our view a bureaucratic-administrative conception, and the subsequent promulgation of a revised but still traditional Code of Civil Law as the fundamental *Gesellschaft*-type legislation affecting all exchange relations among men and enterprises and treating them as instances of a creditor-debtor relationship.[8]

[8] Soviet lawyers, in their public pronouncements at least, would not accept this analysis or the typology on which it is based, though they would concede, we think, that it deals with real problems and real tensions. Their own effort is going, in a reasonably interesting way, into an attempt to develop a much more sophisticated theory of socialist law than the theories propounded by Engels, Vyshinsky or the Communist Chinese – a theory that no longer sees law as exclusively or even primarily a weapon of class rule, at least in socialist societies, but recognises its administrative functions in the ordering of production and distribution and of social and political life. The conception, in fact, involves a mixture of *Gemeinschaft, Gesellschaft* and bureaucratic-administrative strains, each of which is seen as having an appropriate place in Soviet law and in Soviet life, though the lawyers characteristically disagree on the nature of an optimal mix. The recognition of the three strains as a proper part of Soviet life, even if they are not called by the names we have given them, is evident in a great deal of Soviet material and is linked with the official line that representative, participa-

In Communist China, the same trends and tensions are at work, but the *Gemeinschaft* strain has been far stronger; the bureaucratic-administrative strain, while far from absent, has been seriously weakened by the failure of China to embark on massive industrialisation; and the situation is still in flux. The future of law in China, we would argue, depends on the comparative balance and the interrelation of those fundamental strains or 'ideal types' of social regulation that we have attempted to isolate and describe. The same, in an infinitely more complex way, is true of our society. Despite the political differences in economic organisation, social structure and political life – differences that may be overwhelmingly important for culture, for freedom of expression and for the citizen in much of his daily life – in law, east and west may well be set on paths of convergence, or, at the least, of recognising the similarity of many of their problems, thus bringing out, if only implicitly, that the abolition of private property in the means of production, distribution and exchange is not the only real issue of our time and not the fundamental premise from which the solution of all significant social problems immediately follows. Where such abolition has taken place, it has had less effect in removing, or fundamentally altering, the character of social, administrative and legal problems than one might have expected.

---

tory and expert-technical political functions will all have their place even in the ultimately communist society: see, for instance, V. E. Guliev, A. I. Denisov, et al., *Sotsialisticheskoe pravo*, Moscow, 1973 (being Volume 4 of the series *Marksistko-Leninskaya obshchaya teoriya gosudarstva i prava*), pp.437-9; Yu. A. Tikhomirov, 'Vlast' demokratiya, professionalizm', *Sovetskoe gosudarstvo i pravo*, no.1, 1968, p.24; Yu. A Tikhomirov, 'Razdelenie vlastei ili razdelenie truda' in *Sovetskoe gosudarstvo i pravo*, no.1, 1967, p.14 and other writers cited in A. E. S. Tay, 'Gemeinschaft, Gesellschaft, Mobilisation and Administration: The Future of Law in Communist China', *Asia Quarterly*, no.3, 1971, pp.257-303, especially pp.260-75.

Notes on the Contributors

Herbert Enoch Hallam, Professor of Medieval History in the University of Western Australia and a Fellow of the Royal Historical Society, was born in Pembridge, Herefordshire in 1923, and educated at Jesus College, Cambridge, and the University of Nottingham, where he took his doctorate. He taught history at Spalding Grammar School and Loughborough Training College before coming to Western Australia in 1961. His publications include *The New Lands of Elloe* (1954) and *Settlement and Society* (1965); he is editing and contributing to vol.II of the *Agrarian History of England and Wales*.

Crawford Brough Macpherson is Professor of Political Science in the University of Toronto and a Fellow of the Royal Society of Canada. He was born in Toronto in 1911, educated there and at the University of London, and has spent a year as Fellow of Churchill College, Cambridge. He has published numerous articles on political concepts and political theory and has contributed to several collections, among them the Nomos volume on *Revolution* ed. Friedrich (1966); *Philosophy, Politics and Society*, Third series, ed. Laslett and Runciman (1967); and *Social Development* ed. Stanley (1972). His books include *Democracy in Alberta* (1953), *The Political Theory of Possessive Individualism* (1962), *The Real World of Democracy* (1965) and *Democratic Theory: Essays in Retrieval* (1973). He has also edited and contributed to *Property: A Controversy* (1973). During 1973 he was Visiting Fellow in the History of Ideas Unit in the Australian National University.

Eugene Kamenka is Professorial Fellow in the History of Ideas in the Australian National University, a Fellow of the Academy of the Social Sciences in Australia and a Fellow of the Australian Academy of the

Humanities. He was born in Cologne, Germany, in 1928 and educated in Australia at the Sydney Technical High School, Sydney University and the Australian National University. He has worked and taught in Israel, England, the United States and Singapore and has spent a year as a visiting research worker in the Faculty of Philosophy in Moscow State University. His books include *The Ethical Foundations of Marxism* (1962), *Marxism and Ethics* (1969) and *The Philosophy of Ludwig Feuerbach* (1970); he has edited *A World in Revolution?* (1970), *Paradigm for Revolution? – The Paris Commune 1871-1971* (1972), and *Nationalism – The Nature and Evolution of an Idea* (1973). He is currently completing a book on Freudianism and ethics and working on several studies of Marx and aspects of Marxism. During 1973 and 1974 he has also been Visiting Professor in the Faculty of Law of the University of Sydney.

Ronald Stanley Neale, Professor of Economic History in the University of New England, was born in Southall, Middlesex in 1927 and educated at University College, Leicester and Bristol University. He taught history and liberal studies at Bath College of Further Education before coming to New South Wales in 1964. He is the author of *Class and Ideology in the Nineteenth Century* (1972) and has published numerous articles on the economic and social history of England in the eighteenth and nineteenth centuries and contributed to several collections, among them *Rural Change and Urban Growth, 1500-1800*, ed. Chalklin and Havinden (1974) and *Eighteenth Century Studies*, Vol. III, ed. Brissenden, to be published in 1975. He is currently working on an economic and social history of Bath, 1700-1850 and a reconsideration of Marx's position on the English Industrial Revolution. He worked in the History of Ideas Unit in the Australian National University as a Visiting Fellow from November 1973 to February 1974.

John Grenville Agard Pocock is Professor of History and Political Science in Washington University, St Louis, and, during 1973, was Visiting Fellow in the History of Ideas Unit in the Australian National University. He was born in London in 1924 and educated in New Zealand and the University of Cambridge where he took his doctorate in 1952. He has taught at universities in New Zealand and America and has recently spent a year as a Fellow of Churchill College, Cambridge. He has contributed to *Philosophy, Politics and Society*, Second series, ed. Laslett and Runciman (1962), *The Historian's Workshop*, ed. L. P. Curtis Jnr (1970), and *Machiavelli and the Nature of Political Thought*, ed.

Fleisher (1971). His books include *The Ancient Constitution and the Feudal Law* (1957), *Politics, Language and Time* (1971), and *The Machiavellian Moment: Florentine Political Thought and the Atlantic Republican Tradition. A Study in the Politics of Time*, to be published by Princeton University Press. He is currently editing the political writings of James Harrington for Cambridge University Press.

Alice Erh-Soon Tay is Senior Lecturer in Law in the Australian National University. She was born in Singapore in 1934 and educated at Raffles Girls' School, Singapore, the Inns of Court, London, and the Australian National University. She is the author of articles on Soviet law, Chinese communist law, common law and comparative law; she has contributed to the *Encyclopedia of Soviet Law* and is co-author, with Dr Kamenka, of two forthcoming books, *Marxism and the Theory of Law* and *Law*. During 1974 she is also Visiting Professor in the Faculty of Law in the University of Sydney, teaching a course on the socialist contribution to law and legal theory.

Francis James West, a Foundation Fellow and former Secretary of the Australian Academy of the Humanities, is now Dean of Arts and Social Studies in the University College at Buckingham, after having been a Senior Research Fellow, Senior Fellow and Professorial Fellow in the Department of Pacific History of the Australian National University's Research School of Pacific Studies. Born in Hull in 1927, he was educated at Hymers College, the University of Leeds and Trinity College, Cambridge. He has taught at the Victoria University of Wellington and been Professor of Comparative Government in the University of Adelaide at Bedford Park (now Flinders University). His publications include *Political Advancement in the South Pacific* (1961), *Hubert Murray* (1962), *The Justiciarship in England 1066-1232* (1965), *Hubert Murray: Australian Pro-Consul* (1968); he has edited the selected letters of Hubert Murray and is now working on a biography of Murray's brother, Gilbert.

Index

Adair, J., 99 n 22
Addison, Joseph, 80-81
Agreement, Augustan concept of, 75-6
Agriculture
  identification of church year with, 46-7; in eighteenth-
  century ideology of individualism, 81-3; Marx's concept of
  origins of capitalism in, 3, 4, 15-24, 58-9, 88; monastic
  system of, 3-4, 22, 35-46; societies based on, in
  Gemeinschaft types of law, 136-7; as source of capitalism,
  3-4, 18, 40, 91-4; *see also* Country
Albert, William, 94 n 16, 101 n 25
Alienation
  of individual, 20; growth of culture as instrument of, 73-4;
  in contemporary society, 141; reflected in law, 132; of
  property, right of, 7, 99, 100, 106, 109 and n6, 116-7, 137
American Declaration of Independence, 134
Ancient society, Marx's concept of, 13-14, 16, 18
Annenkov, P., 23 n 25
Aquinas, St Thomas, 108
Aristocracy, landed, *see* Landowners
Aristotle, 65, 108, 112, 121
Armies, standing
  Augustan financing of, 71; fear of corruption arising from
  existence of, 69-70, 72-3
Arms, bearing, ownership of
  as service owed for land, 4, 53, 56, 58-9; by bands of
  retainers, 16, 53-4; in relation to concept of civic virtue,
  5-6, 65-9, 72-4
Arts, *see* Culture
Ashley, W.J., 29
Asiatic society, Marx's concept of, 12-13, 15, 16, 18
Augustan period, Augustans
  concept of citizenship, 68-70, 72-6; critique of capitalism,
  63-4, 72-82; critique of society, 68-82; reactions to financial
  revolution, 5, 71-2, 74-6, 82-3; version of radical democracy,
  5, 83
Augustine, St, 49, 108, 112
Ausonius, 58

Babylon, *Gesellschaft* elements in legal system, 141
Bailiffs, medieval, 48-9
Bailyn, B., 83 n 17
Ball, John, 49
Bank of England, significance of founding of, 71
Barbarian attacks against Europe, 15, 30-31, 35, 53, 59
Basil, St, 30
Bath, City of, 93, 97-8, 100
Bath, W. Pulteney, first Earl of, 6, 90, 100
Bath Trust, 101
Beckett, Thomas, 59
Benedict, St, 30-31, 32-3, 49
Benedictine Rule, 30-31, 32-3, 34-5, 38, 45

Benefices
  as form of landholding, 53; feudal fusion of vassalage and,
  54-7; heritability of, 56
Beneficiaries
  rights of, in English land law, 96-101
Beneficium, medieval concepts of *feudum* and, 4, 5, 52-3,
  55-7; origins of terms, 52-3
Bentham, Jeremy, 81, 111 n 9, 113; *see also* Utilitarianism
Bettenson, H, 32 n 3
Bills of Exchange, acceptance as property, 98
Black Book of Peterborough, 40-41
Bodin, Jean, 108
Bolingbroke, H. St John, Viscount, 68
Bolingbroke and His Circle, Kramick, 68 n 4
Bottomore, T.B., 20 n 18
Boulainvilliers, Comte de, 52
Bourgeoisie
  attitudes to economic and social change, 89-90; definition
  of, 68, 85-6 and n 3; influence in changing concept of
  property, 9-10; Marx's concept of rise, role of, 4-5, 24-5,
  51-2, 85, 86-7, 88-90; nineteenth-century commercial, as
  paradigm of *Gesellschaft* law, 142; role in development of
  credit system, industrialisation, 82-3, 90-94, 95-102; role
  in development of *Gesellschaft* law, 137
Bracton, Henry de, 57
Bridgman, Sir Orlando, 100
British Political Elite, The, Guttsman, 91
Brodsky trial, 142
Bubble Act, 95, 101
Bureaucratic-administrative type of law
  characteristics, 7-8, 138, 139-40, 141, 143 and n 8; trend
  towards, in modern society, 142; weakening of, in commu-
  nist China, 144
Burke, Edmund, 68

Canals, significance of investment by landowners in, 93
Capital
  bourgeois attitudes to accumulation of, 89-90; development
  of concept of, as property, 110-12 and n 9; Marx's concept
  of origins, role of, 18-24, 25, 87, 88-9 and n 9; Marx's
  concept of socialisation from within, 139; Marx's theory of
  primary accumulation of, 21-6, 88-9
Capital. Marx, 6, 11, 22-3, 24, 60, 86, 88
Capital Formation in the Industrial Revolution, Crouzet, 89
  n 11
Capitalism, capitalists
  Augustan critique of, 63-4, 72-82; ideology of, 4, 9;
  influence of liberalism in development of, 9, 95, 120-21;
  influence on concepts of property, 105-14; influence on
  nature of society, 51-2, 63-4, 117; origins, characteristics
  of, 3-4, 15, 29-30, 40, 49, 59-60, 91-4, 95-6, 101-2; Marx's
  concepts of origins, characteristics, 4-5, 11-12, 15, 51-2,
  59-60, 63, 86-9; scarcity in, 122-3

Capitulare de Villis, Charlemagne, 36-7
Cassiodorus, 30
Chalklin, C.W., 94 *n 16*
Chambers, J.D., 29
Chandos, J. Brydges, first Duke of, 6, 90
Charity Commissioners for England and Wales, 130-31
Charlemagne, 36-7, 55; estate management in time of, 35-8
Charles V, 34
Charles the Bald, 56
Chaucer, Geoffrey, 48
China
    communist, theories of socialist law, 143 *n 8*, 144; imperial, bases of legal system, 141; traditional concepts of legal procedure, 136
Christianity
    effect of historical nature of, 46-7; materialism in, 35, 49
Church
    identification with medieval rural life, 46-7; as source of capitalism, 45-6, 49; *see also* Monasticism
Cities
    character of, in ancient, Asiatic, Germanic society, 13-14, 16; important to distinguish from towns, 18
Citizenship
    Aristotelian concept of household as basis for, 65, 68; association with landed property, 5, 68, 71-2, 75; association with ownership, bearing of arms, 5-6, 65-9, 72-4; corrupting influence of commerce on, 75-6, 78-9; Marx's view of, in ancient society, 13-14; role of independence and virtue in Augustan concept of, 68-70, 72-6; undermining of liberal democratic ideal of, 118-20, 133-4
Class and Ideology in the Nineteenth Century, Neale, 91 *n 13*
Clocks, significance of development, 3, 33-5
Collected Papers, Maitland, 99-100
Colonial system, and origins of capitalism, 22-3
Columbia University, crisis of 1968, 131-2
Comitatus, concept of, 53-4
Commendation, in feudalism, 54
Commerce
    values of, 5; as corrupting influence on civic morality, 73, 75-6, 78-9; as key to *Gesellschaft* law, 137
Communes
    in ancient, Asiatic society, 13; in Germanic society, 14, 16
Communist Manifesto, Marx, Engels, 24, 25, 85, 86-7
Communist states, contemporary problems of legal ideology in, 129-30, 141-4
Condition of Man, The, Mumford, 31
Cone, Carl B., 91 *n 13*
Contract
    basis of *Gesellschaft* type of law, 137-9; contemporary restriction of, 127
Cooke, C.A., 101 *n 25*
Copa Surisca, 33
Corporations, modern concept of social responsibility of, 130-33 *and n 2*
Corruption
    concept of, in Augustan social critique, 69-70, 72, 75-6, 82-3; Machiavellian theory of, 64-5
Coulton, G.C., 29
Country
    antagonism between town and, 87; role in Marx's theory of division of labour, 15-18, 21, 22, 24; life in medieval times, 46-9; *see also* Agriculture
Cotterell, M., 96 *n 18*
Coward, B., 96 *n 18*
Credit system
    Augustan reaction to, as perception of capitalism, 71-2, 74-82; concept of, as property, 98; Davenant's view of, 76-7; Defoe's view of, 78-80; Marx's theory of, 23-4; fantasy as inherent in, 76-81; Whig attitude to, 80-81
Critique of Political Economy, Contribution to, Marx, 11
Crouzet, F., 89, 94 *n 16*
Culture, growth of, as threat to civic virtue, 73-4
Cunningham, William, 29

D'Arcy v. Allein, 95
Davenant, Charles, 76-8, 79, 81
Davenant v. Hurdis, 95

Davis, L.E., 101 *n 3*
De Donis Conditionalibus, Statute, 109 *n 6*
Defoe, Daniel, 31, 73, 78-81
Democracy
    ideological crisis of liberal, 128-9, 134-5; influence of ideology of, on changing concepts of property, 116-20; origins of Augustan radical, 5, 9, 81-3
Democratic Theory, Macpherson, 105 *n 1*, 122 *n 13*, 124 *n 15*
Denisov, A.I., 144 *n 8*
Dialogue de Scaccario, Richard son of Nigel, 39-40
Dickson, P.G.M., 71 *n 7*
Discovery and colonisation
    role in rise of capitalism, 22-3, 24; influence on trade, 87, 88
Dobb, M., 87, 91-2
Documents of the Christian Church, Bettenson, 32 *n 3*
Domesday Book, 39, 46
Donoghue v. Stevenson, 131, *n 2*
Dugdale, Sir William, 60

Easton, L.D., 20 *n 18*
Economic liberalism, contribution to emergence of capitalism, 95
Economic structure
    Augustan, 70-72, 74-6, 82-3; capitalist, 89-95, 98-101, 106, 108-14; contemporary revolution in, 114-20, 128-33; in communist societies, 143-4; Marx's concept of capitalist, 51-2, 86-9; Marx's theory of influence on law, 12; Marxian models of, 10-27, 58-60, 63-4, 68; medieval, 29-30, 39-40, 46-9, 58-9; of *Gesellschaft* societies, 137-9; pre-capitalist, 108, 110
Economics, derivation and meaning of term, 65, 68
Effects of Civilisation, The, Hall, 14
Egoism *see* Self-interest
Elizabethan World Picture, The, Tillyard, 29
Enclosures; impetus to capitalist agriculture given by, 22, 92-3, 93-4
Encyclopaedia Britannica, 85
Encyclopaedia of the Social Sciences, 85
Engels, F.,
    aims, method and standing as historian, 51, 59-60; concept of feudalism, 51-2, 58-60; theories of socialist law, 143 *n 8*; *see also Communist Manifesto, Germany Ideology*
England
    agriculture in, as source of capitalism, 15-18, 22, 24, 40-49, 88, 91-5; bourgeoisie in, 9, 82, 85-6, 90-91, 95-6; charity organisations in, 130-31; economic transformation and industrialisation of, 22-6, 71-82, 89-94; financial theory and development in, 23-4, 39-40, 45-6, 74-81; land tenure in, 17, 40-46, 57-8, 69, 96-101, 110-12; role of landowners in ideological transformation of, 9, 94-5, 101-2; law reform in, 130-31, 133-4; medieval estate management in 40-55; medieval rural life in, 46-9; property concepts of, in, 71-2, 95, 98, 110-12
Equity of redemption, in English land law, 97
Esprit des Lois, Montesquieu, 81
Essays in Law and History, Holdsworth, 109
Estate management
    of Charlemagne, 36-8; monastic, 38-45; papal, 35-6; significance of, in development of capitalism, 3-4, 39-40, 45-9, 58-9
Étatism
    in contemporary society, 132-3; tension between *Gesellschaft* law and, 8, 136-40, 141
Europe, Western
    end of classical civilisation in, 30-31; foundations in agrarian society, 29-30; source of capitalism in rural society, 3-4, 15-18, 22, 58-9, 88; reasons for economic superiority, 12
Exchange systems, morality of, 74-81
Exchequer, development in England, 39-40
Exploration, *see* Discovery and colonisation

Fancy or fantasy
    Augustan concept of, 74-5; as inherent part of credit system, 76-81

Fee simple tenure, 98-9, 109 *and n 6*
Feudalism
    concepts of, as system of property relationships, 4-5, 9,
    11-12, 15-18, 40, 46, 52, 54-60, 73; *Gemeinschaft*,
    Gesellschaft elements in, 141; Harrington's view of, 66-8;
    Marx's concepts of, 11-12, 15-18, 51-2, 58-60, 68, 86-7, 89;
    historical development of term, 52-4; *see also Feudum*
Feudum
    medieval concepts of *beneficium* and, 4-5, 52-3, 55-7;
    origins of terms, 52-3
Feuerbach, L., 132 *ns 3, 5*
Financial revolution in England
    character and course of, 5-6, 70-71,92-4; Augustan reactions
    to, 71-2, 74-6, 82-3; neo-Harringtonian reactions to, 69-70,
    73-4; relative roles of bourgeoisie, landowners, in, 5-6,
    82-3, 90-94, 101-2; Marx's view of, 22-4
Financial Revolution in England, The, Dickson, 71 *n 7*
Fleisher, M., 64 *n 2*
Fletcher, Andrew, 72-4
Force, Marx's concept of, in society, 23
Freedom, civic *see* Citizenship
French Revolution
    Declaration of the Rights of Man, 134; influence on Marx
    and Engels, 60; socialism as critique of ideology of, 141
Friedman, W., 96 *n 18,* 127

Gasindi, origins, meaning of term, 54
Gemeinschaft type of law
    characteristics, 7-8, 10, 11, 14, 136-7, 138, 140; influence
    on other systems, 142, 144 *and n 8*
German Ideology, The, Marx, Engels, 11, 13, 15, 17, 21, 86,
    87
Germanic society, Marx's concept of, 14-17, 18
Gesellschaft type of law
    characteristics, 7-8, 10, 11, 14, 137-9, 140, 142; impact of
    bureaucratic-administrative systems on, 142; in contem-
    porary crisis of law, legal ideology, 140-41; in legal system of
    Soviet Union, 143 *and n 8*
Girovagi, see Wandering scholars
Godfrey of Crowland, Abbot of Peterborough, 42-4
'Gothic' society, neo-Harringtonian concept of, 69-70, 72-4,
    75
Government *see* State
Grassby, R., 90 *n 12*
Greece, classical
    alienability of property in, 109 *n 6*; concept of civic virtue
    in, 65, 68
Gregory the Great, St, 35-6, 49
Ground rents, titles to, in English law, 97-8
Grundrisse, The, Marx, 6, 11, 13, 14, 15, 16, 17, 20, 26, 87-8,
    and n 9
Gruner, S., 86 *n 3*
Guddat, K.H., 20 *n 18*
Guest, A.G., 139 *n 7*
Guilds, role in challenge to feudalism, 51-2
Guliev, V.L., 144 *n 8*
Guttsman, W.L., 91
Gwassawl, origins, meaning of term, 54; *see also* Vassal

Hale, Sir Matthew, Lord Chief Justice, 96
Hall, Charles, 14
Hallam, H.E., 3-4, 5, 6, 9, 10
Hamilton, Alexander, and Hamiltonian concept of history, 83
Hardwicke, P. Yorke, first Earl of, 97
Harrington, James, 66-9, 72-3
Harris, D.R., 139 *n 7*
Hartley, D., 81
Hereditaments, corporeal, incorporeal, distinguished, 110 *n 7*
Highland clearances, and origins of wage labour, 22
Hirschman, Albert O., 89
History of English Law, A, Holdsworth, 96 *n 18,* 99-100
Hobbes, Thomas, 81, 123 *and n 14*
Hobsbawn, E.J., 86
Holdsworth, Sir William, 96 *n 18,* 99-100, 109 *n 6*
Holland, property — power relations in seventeenth century, 67

Household
    Aristotelian concept of, as basic for civic personality, 65,
    68; as paradigm of private property, 132-3; agrarian, as key
    to *Gemeinschaft* society, 136-7; in Harrington's doctrine
    of property and power, 68
Humanism, civic, Machiavellian transmission of, 64-5
Hume, David, 81, 108, 111 *n 9*
Husbandry, convertible, development of, 92-3

Income, concepts of property as right to, 7, 67-8, 96-101,
    105-6, 110-12, 114-16
Independence and Augustan concept of civic virtue, 68-70, 72-6
Individualism
    as basis of *Gesellschaft* law, 8, 137-40; eighteenth-century
    ideology of, 64-5, 81-2, 83, 141; contemporary cult of,
    132; subordination in bureaucratic-administrative systems,
    139-41
Industrial law, public character of, 134, 139
Industrial Revolution, 4, 6, 24, 25, 29, 40, 101-2, 141;
    see also Industrialisation
Industrialisation
    effect on concepts of property, 114-16, 139; and Marxian
    theories of labour and capital, 18-21, 24-6; in England
    relative contributions of bourgeoisie, landowners to; 89-
    94; use of trusts in financing, 101
Inheritance
    of benefices, 56; in English land law, 96-101, 109-10 *and*
    ns 6, 7; in Harrington's doctrine of property and power,
    68-9; in Roman law, 110 *n 7*; partible, 41
Institutions of Private Law, The, Renner, 21
Introduction to the History of English Land Law, An,
    Simpson, 96, 97
Introduction to the Principles of Morals and Legislation,
    Bentham, 111 *n 9*
Investment
    by landowners, contribution to capitalism through, 93-4,
    100-101; concept of civic morality of, 77-8, 80-81; as right
    to revenue, 114-15
Iron manufacture, investment by landowners in, 93
Isaac ben Sid, Rabbi, 34
Ives, E.W., 96 *n 18*

James II, 70
Jefferson, Thomas, and Jeffersonian ideal of individual liberty,
    119; Jeffersonian concept of history, 83
Jews, as moneylenders in England, 45; expulsion of, from
    England, 45
Jocelyn of Brakelond, 45
Jones, E.L., 93 *n 15*
Jones, Richard, 12, 14

Kamenka, E., 7-8, 10, 11, 132 *n 5,* 136 *n 6*
Kerridge, E., 93 *n 15*
Kosminsky, E.A., 58
Kramnick, I., 68
Krushchev, N., de-Stalinisation campaign, 143

Labour
    agricultural-Marxian, monastic, physiocratic, Roman views
    of, 17; 32, 35, 38; 87-8; 15, 31-2; Marx's concept of division
    of, 15-17, 18, 21, 24; Marx's view of role in, primary
    accumulation of capital, 21-2, 88; property as access to
    means of, 7, 115-20, 124; property as justification of,
    incentive to, 7, 106, 109, 112-14, 116; slave, in ancient
    society, 13-14; surplus, distinction between absolute,
    relative, 25-6; wage, as component of capital, 18-22, 88;
    see also Industrial law
Land
    alienation of, 7, 99, 100, 106, 109 *and n 6*; appropriation
    of, and origins of wage labour, 22, *see also* Enclosures;
    Marx's concept of relation of property rights to origins
    of modern capital, 87, 88 *and n 9*; repository of property
    and power in Harrington's doctrines, 66-8; significance of
    historical development of rights, in England, 96-102;
    taxation of, 6, 71; *see also* Feudalism, Land tenure, Land-
    owners, Property

Land tenure
feudal systems of, 4, 36, 38, 40-42, 45, 53, 54-8, 73; in
England, 92, 95-100, 109 and n 6, 110 and n 7; Marx's
concept of feudal, 16-17
Landowners
contribution to development of capitalism in England 6,
92-4; in medieval economy, 40, 46, 58-9; and industrialisation, 6, 90-94; Marx's view of feudal, 17, 58; origins of
property law in needs of, 95-102; rights in English land
law, 7, 96-101, 106, 109-10 and ns 6, 7; role in emergence
of radical democracy, 5, 9, 101-2
Law
as reflection of social philosophy, 94-6, 128-36; as agent
of social justice, 128-32; emergence of new areas of, 127-8,
133-4;(Gemeinschaft, Gesellschaft, bureaucratic-administrative
types distinguished, 135-44; Marx's concept of relation
with economy, 12; Marxist view of changes in,
135; nature of current crisis in ideology, 127-30, 133-6,
140-41; and property in England, 6, 95-102, 109-10 and ns
6, 7; role in social and economic change, 9-10, 26, 93-4,
130-44
Law Commissions, in England, 133-4
Lectures on the Principles of Political Obligation, Green, 113
Le Mans, Count of, 56
Lennard, Reginald, 46 and n 7
Levellers, 112
Leviathan, Hobbes, 123 n 14
Liberalism
aspects of, in Augustan ideology, 9, 81-3; contemporary
crisis in, 128-9; importance of economic, in emergence of
capitalism, 95
Licensing laws, in bureaucratic-administrative systems, 139 and n 7
Life tenancies, in English land law, 96-7, 98
Livy, 31
Llandeilo, 48-9
Locke, John, 14, 64, 70, 71, 74-5, 76, 95, 98, 101, 112, 113,
116, 123 n 14
Louis the Pious, 55
Lowther, Sir James, 99

Mabillon, Jean, 60
Machiavelli, N., 64-6, 78, 82
Machiavellian Moment, The, Pocock, 64
McLellan, D., 88 n 8
Macpherson, C.B., 6-7, 9, 10, 67, 74, 95 n 17, 105 n 1, 122 n
13, 123 n 14, 125 n 15
Madox, Thomas, 60
Maitland, F.W., 99-100
Malthus, T., 88 .
Mandeville, B. de, 79, 81
Manorial system, origins of capitalism in, 58-60
Markets, market societies
and changes in concept of property, 110-12 and n 9;
changing character of, 117; influence on feudalism, 4, 59;
alienability of property in, 109-10 and n 6
Marx, Karl
aims, method and standing as historian, 10-12, 51, 59-60;
doctoral dissertation, 20 and n 15; letter to Annenkov, 23,
n 25; see also titles of individual works by Marx, entries
relating to Marx under subject headings, e.g. Bourgeoisie,
Feudalism, Labour, etc., and passim
Materialism
in Christian tradition, 3, 49; materialist view of history, 10
Matrimonial law, basis of contemporary changes, 134
Medieval Latin Lyrics, Waddell, 32 and n 4
Merchant, role of, in development of capitalism, 29, 49, 68-9,
72, 74, 82
Military service see Arms, bearing, ownership of
Militia, 72-3
Mill, J.S., 113
Mineral extraction, investment by landowners in, 93
Mingay, G.E., 94 n 16
Monasteries, monasticism
agricultural practice in, 35-46, 48; as refuge from turmoil
of dark ages, 30-31; contribution to development of
capitalism, 3-4, 29, 40, 49; dissolution of, 22, 46; see also
Benedictine Rule

Money
development of credit system, 70-72, 74-81, 82, 98;
medieval attitude to, 39-40; medieval systems of account-
ing, 39, 46, 47-8; role of, in primary accumulation of
capital, 22-4
Monopolies, Statute of, 95
Montesquieu, C.L. de S., baron de, 79, 81
Moore, D.C., 91 n 13
Moraźe, C., 85-6
Morgan, J.P., 131 n 2
Mortgages, development in England, 97-8
Mumford, Lewis, 29, 31

National Debt, and origins of capitalism in England, 23, 71,
75, 90
Nature, end of man's dependence on, in Marx's theory of
capital, 21
Navigation laws, 93
Navy, significance of, in industrialisation of England, 93
Neale, R.S., 5-6, 9, 10, 90-91, 101 n 25
Neo-Harringtonianism, 69-74
New Model Army, 69, 70
North, D.C., 101 n 25
Nottingham, H. Finch, first Earl of, 97
Noyes, C.R., 110 n 7, 111 n 9

Origins of Modern English Society, The, Perkin, 91, 94, 95
Oxford Essays in Jurisprudence, Guest, 139 n 7

Papacy, role of, in origins of capitalism, 3, 35-6
Pappenheim, Matthäus von, 60
Participation
political, 66, 74; social, 122; in current ideology, 129,
130-32 and n 4
Pashukanis, E.B., 135, 139
Passion, as component of credit mechanism, 76-81
Patronage, Augustan view of, as agent of corruption, 69-70, 72
Peasants, position of, in medieval England, 46, 48-9
Pelagius, 49
Pepin the Short, 37-8
Perkin, H., 90-91, 93, 94, 95
Peter of Maricourt, 33
Peterborough, Abbey of, 42-4, 48
Petty, Sir William, 23
Physiocrats, concept of source of wealth, 87-8
Plato, 31, 108
Plumb, J.H., 90-91
Pocock, J.G.A., 5, 6, 9, 10, 64 ns 1, 2, 69 n 5, 83 n 17
Political Theory of Possessive Individualism, The, Macpherson,
67, 95, 123 n 14
Politics, Language and Time, Pocock, 64 n 2
Polyptique d'Irminon, 38
Polyptiques, as origin of medieval ecclesiastical accounting
system, 35-6
Pope, Alexander, 80
Popper, K., 133
Portland, W.H. Cavendish Bentinck, third Duke of, 99
Possession, legal concept of, 139 n 7
Principles of Political Economy, Mill, 113
Productivity, in Marx's theory of capital, 21, 25-6
Property
concepts, definitions of, 4-7, 95, 97-8, 105-6, 114-16, 117,
122-3; and labour, 7, 25-6; 112-16, 118-20; and origins of
capitalism, 11-12, 21, 95; and society, 7, 10, 13-14, 116-
20, 121-4, 130-33 and n 2; and state, 107, 114-15, 117-20,
144; as moral issue, 5, 65-9, 72-4, 106, 108, 112; as power,
7, 66-9, 120-21; as right to material things, 110-12; as right
to revenue, 96-101, 108-10, 114-16; common, 12-15, 106-8;
in Gemeinschaft, Gesellschaft, bureaucratic-administrative
law, 137-8, 139; liberal ideologies of, 5, 112-14, 119-20,
121-3; private, 12-15, 21, 108-10, 133; private, as basis of
feudalism, 16-17, 52, 54-7; alienation of private, 100,
108-10, 116-17; see also Inheritance
Property, Macpherson, 106 n 2
Protestant ethic, 29, 80-81
Pulteney, William, see Bath, W. Pulteney, first Earl of

Pulteney, William Johnstone, later Sir W., 100
Pulteney Estate Papers, Bath, 100

Quia Emptores, Statute of, 109 *n 6*

Radicalism, in eighteenth and nineteenth centuries, 91
Railways, legislation concerning, 138
Real Property, Topham, 110 *n 7*
Reeves *see* Bailiffs
Reform Bill of 1832, 91
Regularis Concordia, 33
Reich, C., 115 *n 12*
Religion, influence of, in *Gemeinschaft* law, 136
Renner, K., 21, 135, 136-7
Rentier, role of, in capitalism, 6, 72, 74, 90, 114
Republicanism, classical, Machiavellian transmission of, 64-5
Review, The, 78-80
Revolution of 1688 in England, 70
Rheims, Archbishop of, 56
Ricardo, D., 88
Richard, son of Nigel, 39
Ritual, in *Gemeinschaft* law, 136
Robert the Englishman, 33-4
Robinson Crusoe, Defoe, 31
Robson, R., 91 *n 13*
Roman law
    alienability of property in, 109 *n 6*; concept of *res* in, 110
    n 7; *Gesellschaft* strains in, 141
Rome, ancient
    concept of *comitatus* in, 53-4; Marx's view of, 13-14; status
    of agricultural labour in, 31-2; theories on rise, fall of, 15,
    30, 31-2, 65, 72
Rostow, W.W., 11, 89
Rousseau, J.J., 73, 79, 81

Saint-Simon, C.H. de R., comte de, 141
Scarcity, influence on concepts of property, 122-3
Schwoerer, L.G., 73, *n 8*
Self-interest, rational, theories of, 81-2
Serfdom, 38, 46, 48, 58; Marx's view of, 16-17, 58, 86-7
Sheridan, L.A., 131 *n 1*
Simpson, A.W.B., 96 *n 18*, 97
Slavery, 32, 36, 54; Marx's view of, 13, 18
Smith, Adam, 87
Snape, R.H., 46
Social pressure, as element in *Gemeinschaft* law, 136-7, 142
Social responsibility as phenomenon of contemporary society,
    114-15, 118, 130-32
Socialism
    ideology of law in, 8, 128-30, 135, 141; revolutionary, as
    radical critique of society, 91, 116, 128-9, 140-41
Society
    Augustan critique of, 68, 83; contemporary revolution in,
    128-34, 142; Marx's critique of capitalist, 86-9; Marx's
    models of ancient, Asiatic, Germanic, 12-14, 16-17;
    medieval, 29-49; medieval, contrasted with Marxian model,
    55-9
Sombart, Werner, 105
Soviet Union
    legal system in, 129-30, 142-3; operational management in,
    139
Spectator, The, Addison, 80-81
Spelman, Sir H., 60
Stages of Economic Growth, The, Rostow, 11, 89
Stapleton, Thomas, 41 *n 6*
State
    as guarantor of income, 7, 114-15; as regulator of law,
    society, 7-8, 128-30, 132-6; 138-40, 142-3; as regulator of
    property, labour, 114-16, 117-20; role in development of
    Augustan capitalism, 70-74
Stewart, Gilbert, 14
Stockholders, stockjobbers, role in credit system, 6, 72, 74, 75
Stourzh, G., 83 *n 17*
Sweezy, P.M., 87, 92
Swiss Family Robinson, The, Wyss, 31

Tacitus, 31, 53
Tawney, R.H., 3, 4, 29, 105

Taxation
    contribution of, to development of capitalism, 23, 71, 93,
    120; of land, 6, 71
Tay, A.E. –S., 7-8, 10, 11, 136 *n 6*, 144 *n 8*
Technology
    role in development of capitalism, 89-90, 93; Marx's view
    of, 25-6; social consequences of revolution in, 133-4
Tenants Law, 98-9
Theories of Surplus Value, Marx, 23
Thirsk, Joan, 93 *n 15*
Tikhomirov, Yu. A., 144 *n 8*
Tillyard, E.M.W., 29
Timber production, landowners' investment in, 93
Time, influence of Benedictine attitude to, 3, 32-5
Tönnies, F., 135, 136-7
Topham, A.F., 110 *n 7*
Tories, attitudes to credit system, commerce, 76, 83
Tort, law of, changing contemporary position of, 127, 134
Towns
    antagonism between country and, 87; important to
    distinguish from cities, 18; role in Marx's theory of division
    of labour, 15-18, 21, 22; as source of change in feudal
    society, 59
Trade
    as possible cause of decline of feudalism, 59, 87; Augustan
    attitude to, 75, 78-9, 82; in Marx's view of bourgeoisie,
    86-7, 90
Treatise of Human Nature, Hume, 111 *n 9*
Treatises of Government, Two, Locke, 70, 75, 98, 101, 123 *n*
Trenchard, John, 72-4
Triumph of the Middle Classes, The, Morazé, 85-6
True-Born Englishman, The, Defoe, 73 *n 9*
Trusts, in English law, 96-7, 99-101
Tucker, Robert, 86 *n 3*
Turnpikes
    investment by landowners in, 93; trust development of, 101

United States of America
    constitution, 74 *and n 10*, 134; revolution, causes of, 83
Urbanisation, investment by landowners in, 93
Use, concept of, in English law, 96-9
Uses, Statute of, 96
Usury
    as characteristic of Marxian capitalism, 23-4; in medieval
    England, 45; in Augustan England, 74-5, 78
Utilitarianism, and the welfare ideology, 128

Vaines, J.C., 111 *n 9*
Vassal, vassalage
    as characteristic institution of feudal society, 54-7; origins,
    meaning of term, 54
Villa, organisation of Carolingian, 36-8
Viner, J., 105
Virtue
    in Augustan concept of citizenship, 5, 66-70, 72-6, 81-2;
    Machiavellian concept of, 64-6
Vyshinsky, A. Ya., 143 *n 8*

Waddell, H., 32
Wage contracts, significance of, in Marx's theory of capitalism,
    20-21
Wage Labour and Capital, Marx, 18
Wall Street Journal, 131 *n 2*
Walter of Whittlesey, 42-4
Wandering scholars, 31
Ward, J.T., 94 *n 16*
Weber, Max, 3, 4, 11, 12, 29, 89, 105, 135
West, F.J., 4-5, 6, 9, 10
Western society, crisis of legal ideology in, 129-30
Whigs, attitudes to credit system, commerce, 76, 80-81, 83
William the Conqueror, 39, 73; *see also* Domesday Book
William of Woodford, abbot of Peterborough, 42
Wills, Statute of, 96
Wilson, R.G., 94 *n 16*
Wood, G.S., 83 *n 17*

Yale, D.E.C., 96 *n 18*

'Zur Judenfrage', Marx, 20